The Warsaw Underground

A Memoir of Resistance, 1939–1945

by
JAN ROSINSKI
with
RICHARD HILE

McFarland & Company, Inc., Publishers
Jefferson, North Carolina, and London

All photos courtesy Dr. Grazyna Anna Kras.

LIBRARY OF CONGRESS CATALOGUING-IN-PUBLICATION DATA

Rosinski, Jan, 1917–2012.
    The Warsaw underground : a memoir of resistance,
1939–1945 / by Jan Rosinski with Richard Hile.
       p.   cm.
    Includes bibliographical references and index.

    ISBN 978-0-7864-7693-0
    softcover : acid free paper ∞

    1. Rosinski, Jan, 1917–2012. 2. World War, 1939–1945—
Underground movements—Poland—Warsaw. 3. Poland.
Polskie Siły Zbrojne. Armia Krajowa—Biography.
4. Government, Resistance to—Poland—Warsaw—History—
20th century. 5. World War, 1939–1945—Personal
narratives, Polish. 6. Warsaw (Poland)—Biography.
7. Warsaw (Poland)—History, Military—20th century.
I. Hile, Richard, 1937– II. Title.
D765.2.W3R66 2014
940.53'43841092—dc23
[B]   2013034975

BRITISH LIBRARY CATALOGUING DATA ARE AVAILABLE

On the cover: Polish Underground Army armbands worn by Jan
Rosinski and his wife Barbara during the 1944 Uprising; grunge
frame iStockphoto/Thinkstock

Manufactured in the United States of America

McFarland & Company, Inc., Publishers
  Box 611, Jefferson, North Carolina 28640
  www.mcfarlandpub.com

In loving memory of my wife, Barbara
— *Jan Rosinski*

In respectful memory of author Jan Rosinski,
who did not live to see his story in print.
He became an inspiration to all
who knew him in time of war,
and thereafter through the discoveries he made
in the field of atmospheric science
— *Richard Hile*

Acknowledgments

The authors, and especially Jan Rosinski, owe much to the support, given daily, by Dr. Grazyna Anna Kras to the work of researching and recording the story of Jan's years in the Warsaw underground. As a medical doctor, she was able to care for the health and welfare of Jan daily and to encourage him to reach back in his memory to 70 some years ago and record on tape his daily existence under the heel of the German occupation of the Polish capital. She also accompanied him on two trips to Poland, in 2000 and 2008, and was instrumental in rescuing him from a stroke on the last visit.

We also wish to thank the assistance given by the Defence Information Services of the British Defence Staff of the British Embassy in Washington, D.C. Through their guidance, we were able to retrieve Jan's military records in the Polish Forces under British command from the Polish Records Office of the Ministry of Defence in Middlesex, UK.

Eileen Kent, of Alexandria, Virginia, volunteered her services as manuscript editor and especially grammarian for a period of history with which she was not entirely familiar. We thank her for her patience in guiding the fledgling efforts of two first-time writers.

Table of Contents

Preface

For Jan Rosinski, the invasion of Poland by Nazi Germany in 1939 was a catastrophic event that propelled him, and fellow students, into the underground movement that was the Polish Home Army (*Armia Krajowa*). This is the firsthand story of those years.

I was friends with Jan for more than 25 years; and when I learned of his experience as a young man in the wartime underground of Poland, I urged him for many years to record his story. Those discussions eventually led to this collaboration. We worked together over a period of two years, Jan recording his memories on several tapes, which he shared with me. Additionally, I conducted two lengthy interviews with him at his home. Many phone calls were made to clarify details and add background. As a lifelong student of history, it was a pleasure to immerse myself in further research on the period.

I welcome this opportunity to record Jan's experiences so that one more untold story of extraordinary heroism during a pivotal time in history can be revealed. In the pages that follow, Jan tells that story.

Richard Hile

Prologue

It has been nearly 70 years since the dark shadow of war descended over Poland and the beginning of World War II in Europe. Two invasions, the first from the west by German forces and the second from the east by the Soviet Red Army, left the country in ruins and its people decimated by the most inhuman acts man could devise. This shadow was not lifted until the communist regime was cast aside with the establishment of a new Poland, the "Third Republic," in December 1989. This long awaited event was followed by the collapse of the Soviet Union in 1991. Yet, during the years of war and occupation, the heartbeat of the country remained: in the underground movement — the Home Army, or *Armia Krajowa* (AK). By 1944, it was the largest resistance organization in Europe. My own role as a university student operative was one of many small parts making up the whole. My life then may sound adventurous now, but it was a life on the edge every waking moment. A wrong turn on a street suddenly controlled by a German patrol or an indiscretion or the turning of a fellow cell member would have meant capture and death.

I was once asked what kept me sane during those underground years. For me, it was my future wife, Barbara, a gifted surgeon known by her AK code name "Basia," and my cat, who was always there and always waiting when I returned home safe from the streets of occupied Warsaw.

America has given me and my family safe haven and a rewarding life in scientific research. Perhaps this book, in some small way, can add to the historical fabric of this welcoming country.

Jan Rosinski • AK Code Name "Halszka"
Boulder, Colorado • July 12, 2008

CHAPTER 1

Invasion

On Friday, September 1, 1939, Americans on the East Coast awoke to radio news reports from London that the German army had crossed the Polish frontier in massive strength at three points, launching the outbreak of World War II in Europe. We in Poland had been at war for six hours, and already our military and civilian casualties were mounting. The German invasion would also introduce the world to *Blitzkrieg* (lightning war) and I would soon have a chance meeting with the man responsible for its creation and execution.

That same morning, little did I know I would be starting a journey into the spearhead of the northern attack route through East Prussia and then to the underground resistance movement. As an advanced chemistry student, I had just finished a summer work program, sponsored by my school, the Warsaw Institute of Technology, at the German-owned Zeumer chemical plant in Katowice in Upper Silesia. It had been an enjoyable and rewarding experience, particularly being on my own, and I had been well compensated for my work in the plant laboratory. Preferably forgotten was my required work activity report submitted to the chemistry faculty of the Warsaw Institute of Technology for review. I had made the error of mentioning in my report that I had enjoyed playing tennis as much as I had enjoyed my work. The report failed to pass the reviewers' scrutiny.

Playing tennis did provide one enjoyable diversion, however, and that was my challenging matches with Hilda, an attractive German woman and resident of Katowice. They were enjoyable until I was informed by my company boss, Dr. Huppert, that Hilda was married and that her husband was a German Gestapo (*Geheimpolizei*) officer. Sometime during heated volleys, she would call out, "We will crush Poland!" And I would reply, "When the war is over, you won't be able to get a job washing dishes in our house!" As fate would have it, in the next few years to come, both she and I would have at least one opportunity to save each other from capture.

A taxi arrived at my apartment in Katowice, the driver already nervous, with bombing in the distance. Loading my suitcase into the car, I told the driver I needed to go back, thinking I might have left something behind. I found nothing, except a bottle of fine Russian cognac in a pantry cupboard. I grabbed the bottle and off we went to the central train station for my return trip home to Warsaw. As the taxi sped through Katowice, already congested with confused and panicky civilians, public loudspeakers demanded that city authorities surrender to the German command. Infiltrators in a fifth column already among us and only three hours into the invasion!

When I arrived at the station at eight o'clock that morning, crowds were already clamoring for an escape route away from the conflict. Lugging my suitcase, with tennis racket sticking out and the cognac in the other hand, there was nothing I could do but sit on a platform bench and figure out just what to do next. I had just missed a train departing for Warsaw, but getting aboard would have been hopeless anyway. The first refugees of the war were hanging from windows and doorways, while others clung to the roofs of cars as the train pulled out of the station. The stationmaster approached, a kindly fellow, as luck would have it, clearly eying the bottle of cognac resting on the bench next to me. He could see, by the school cap I was wearing, that I was a student and perhaps worth rescuing. "What have you there?" he asked, with obvious intent. "Let's have a drink!" He joined me on the bench, which led to conversation, interspersed with a few nips of cognac. He informed me that the train I had just missed would be the last one of the day for Warsaw. "Well," I said, "I'll just wait here forever, if necessary. I can't commit suicide." We agreed that this war was not starting off very well and that it likely would be over in three or four days. So why not relax and watch history go by? Soon thereafter, an unexpected announcement blared from the platform speaker that an international express train would be arriving momentarily en route from Prague to Warsaw. This was news to the stationmaster and an unexpected opportunity for me. Although I had a ticket for a lesser class train, he volunteered to see me aboard to a first class compartment. He wished me a safe journey, and I expressed my hope for his survival. Waving good-bye from my compartment window, I was happy with my first class accommodations, and he with my bottle of cognac in his possession.

The rail distance to Warsaw was about 300 kilometers, which normally would have set my arrival at Warsaw's central station late the same afternoon. The trip, however, was not without incident. The train was attacked at least twice by the Luftwaffe's Stuka dive bombers. Both fortunately were misses, with the bombs falling alongside the tracks but at a distance that caused no more damage than some blown-out windows. We had all heard about the fearsome scream of the Stukas as they dived on their targets, but I, perhaps in my false bravado, did not think them so fearful. Later we would learn that the Ju.87 Junkers were equipped with air brakes. To add psychological warfare to the diving attack, the pilot would manipulate the brake controls to produce the banshee noise. These and other interruptions along the way, including unscheduled stops, turned the trip into an overnight journey.

On the train's arrival at Warsaw station the next morning, the Luftwaffe was making its first bomb runs over the city. Fortunately, I was able to get out of the station before the train was heavily damaged. I immediately ran from the station to the apartment at Marszalkowska Street 95 in the city center, where I lived with my mother. I had called her from Katowice to inform her of my travel, but she was still wrought with worry over my late return. She greeted me as any fretting mother would, and then handed me a notice of my induction into the Polish armed forces and a summons to report to a reception center in a border area far to the northeast of Warsaw and away from an invasion route. She told me that my first cousin Slawomir Giedroyc, a fellow WIT student in mechanical engineering, had also received his induction notice and was waiting to hear from me. As I was older than Slawomir, if only a few months, it was time for me for form a plan and head my "first command" of two green draftees. Overlooked in this simple hierarchy was my cousin's claim to "noble" birth as the son born into a family whose ancestors were the direct descendants of the Duke of Lithuania. Bohdan, his father, and Jan, his grandfather, were still looked upon as noblemen and were well regarded in Polish society.

Early on the morning of September 3, I made a decision on the spot to leave that afternoon for the army reception center. Suddenly, later that day, word reached the citizens of Warsaw from BBC broadcasts that England had finally honored its defense treaty with Poland and declared war against Germany. I and several friends joined the crowds on the main boulevards surging toward the British embassy, which occupied the Count Branicki Palace at No. 18 Nowy Swiat. Makeshift Polish and British flags were unfurled and anthems sung by the overjoyed crowd. When the British ambassador emerged on a balcony to greet us, the crowd erupted again. What a joyous moment! We all thought now Germany would be defeated

for sure! Soon thereafter, a second celebration arose when reports came
that France had also declared war on Germany. The Allies were on their
way. Yet as the hours and days passed with no military action, a sense of
foreboding would spread across the land. The Allied inaction would later
be labeled the "Phony War."

However, now with spirits still high, and knowing it would be a long
journey, it was time for us to set out. We would have to travel light, so no
backpack or bed roll, and food would have to be scavenged along the way.
I changed my dress shoes to climbing boots, took my hat, and bid good-
bye to my mother. It was an emotional parting, as we both knew that the
deadly winds of war could blow our way. She had endured many ordeals
in her younger years, as we, almost in another life, were refugees from the
October Revolution in Russia.

I first made my way to join up with Slawomir at his family's house
on Hoza Street, also in the city center. Saying good-byes to my aunt Zofia
and her family, we then set out on our journey, which would take me, at
least, on a circuitous route over 23 days, ending back in Warsaw the day
before the Polish military command surrendered to the German army.
Recollection, in detail, of days on the road and specific events have since
faded from my memory. Each day merged into another. Most disturbing,
then and now, is that somehow my cousin and I became separated and his
disappearance was a mystery at that time. Years later, during one of my
visits in Warsaw after the war, his brother, Leszek, told me that Slawomir
had somehow survived the war. Recently, I got some information about
him from his son, Jan Giedroyc. After the Warsaw Uprising, Slawomir, as
a displaced person, moved from Warsaw to the south of Poland — Szymbark
near Gorlice — where he got married just before the end of war in 1945.
Soon thereafter, he moved with his wife and son, Jan, to the small town
of Walim in the region of Sudety, where his father opened a pharmacy
after the war. During that time, Slawomir finished his education, which
had been interrupted by the war, at the Institute of Technology in Gliwice
in Upper Silesia, while working at the same time for the Project Office of
Chemical Industry, ERG. Around 1953 he returned together with his family to Warsaw, where he had worked as a mechanical engineer for the war
industry. In 1964 he moved again because of his job to the town of Jaslo
in southern Poland, where he would spend the rest of his life. He died in
1983 before he could finally see a new Poland freed from so many years of
communism. Yet, it was difficult for me to accept that I never heard from
him again.

Meanwhile, my second cousin Leszek, two years younger than Slawek, worked at the tobacco factory and later as conductor of Suburban Shuttle Electric Train, EKD, in occupied Warsaw. After the war he graduated from the Department of Pharmacy at the University of Warsaw. First, he worked for the State Chamber of Commerce in Warsaw and then as a chief of the Department of Scientific and Technical Information of the Vaccines and Serums Factory in Warsaw. He spent most of his life in Warsaw and passed away in February 2006, survived by his wife, Maria, and two children, Elzbieta and Witold.

In one incident early in our journey together, Slawomir and I were passing through a dense forested area. Huddled in the trees was a young couple with a baby, who was crying and obviously in pain. The mother was distraught and asked if we could help with medicine. We had nothing to offer, but after talking it over, we came up with a plan. A short time earlier, we had passed through a small town and noticed a pharmacy. We walked back to the town and found the pharmacy closed, as it was already evening. We decided to take a risk and break in. No point in finessing it, so Slawomir kicked in the door. We quickly rifled through the shelves and selected the more obvious medicines, especially for fever, and dumped them into a small box. Slawomir's father was a pharmacist, so he had some exposure to medications and their uses. We made our way back to the family, gave them the medicines and began to look for a place to bed down for the night.

Suddenly, we heard voices — German voices — and saw shadows moving through the forest. This appeared to be a small patrol, and there wasn't much discipline in their movement, as they were telling jokes and laughing. This was a perfect opportunity for an ambush, had we been armed. I had acquired some skill as a marksman with a rifle, and had some experience in shooting competitions. Luckily for the patrol, they passed unharmed. Then we ran into a squad of Polish soldiers not far from where we sighted the German troops. I asked them who their commanding officer was, and a sergeant replied, "Stanislaw Rosinski." To this day, I cannot believe I had a total mental block in associating my uncle Stanislaw with this army patrol. (There were three uncles on my father's side of the family, and Jan and the others were all involved in some military or resistance activity during World War I or World War II. Even within the family, none of us spoke of it openly, as it was best to protect the family's security by maintaining some degree of compartmentation of our individual activities. Nevertheless, our paths would cross occasionally over the next six years.) Slawomir and I met the Polish troops close to an unoccupied forester's cabin. They told us it would be safe to stay there overnight and gave us something to drink. This was a rare opportunity to have a roof over our heads. A few days later, we ran into another Polish army patrol, and were warned that if we continued to walk in a northerly direction, we would run into the Russian army. It was September 17 and the Red Army had just invaded Poland from the east, sealing off any route of retreat from the German army.

For the first time on this trek, confusion clouded our thinking. The realization set in that our efforts to report, as ordered, to the designated induction center would fail. Also, it was at about this time that somehow Slawomir and I became separated. I do not recall whether we were still together when the next day brought an unexpected encounter with the German army, the *Wehrmacht*. As night approached, I fell exhausted into a roadside ditch next to an orchard and immediately fell into a deep sleep. At daybreak, I awoke suddenly to strange noises. Foggy with sleep, I jolted upright and found myself not five feet from a line of German heavy tanks, with all their engines idling. The lead tank was fronted by motorcycle security escorts, and a long line of tanks, armored vehicles and trucks followed to the rear.

Near me, one officer sitting on the turret of the lead tank laughingly called out, "Well look, he's actually alive!" Others laughed as I came to my feet.

"Good morning," I said in my best school *Volksdeutsche*.

"Good morning," he replied, smiling slightly. "Are you hungry?"

"No. Well maybe a little, but I'll survive," I answered.

"Don't worry, we won't poison you," again a smile. "Would you like some tea?"

"All right, thank you," I replied, as I approached the tank.

Just then, an open command car with a complement of senior officers pulled up in front of the tank. The obviously senior officer stepped out and walked over to me.

"What is this cap you're wearing?" he asked.

"My school. I am Jan Rosinski, Warsaw Institute of Technology. And who are you?"

And to this day, I'll never forget his simple reply: "Guderian."

"Oh, I've heard about you fighting in Spain ... the civil war."

"Yes, that's right," he acknowledged.

"Tell me," he asked, "how could you possibly sleep through the battle that just went on in the village down the road?"

I replied simply that I'd been so exhausted that I would have slept through an earthquake.

Then, he looked straight at me and said, "The Polish force we fought against in that village was commanded by a Rosinski. We captured him three times, and each time, he was able to escape when his soldiers rescued him." As I later learned, this was my uncle Stanislaw, but at that moment, I was too confused and avoided replying to his comment. (The remainder of this story comes later.)

Then, Guderian asked, "Do you happen to know Dr. Reppe?"

"I know of him, of course, he's a very famous chemist, but I've not met him personally."

"Are you a good student at your institute?"

Not lacking modesty, for I was an honors student, I immediately answered, "Yes, the best!"

"Well then, perhaps you can work for us someday ... to help the Third Reich. So, you and your friends must go back to school and finish your studies, and together, we'll do it."

"Perhaps." I hesitated, thinking we appeared to be losing the war already.

I was then offered some food, which I declined, claiming I had some bread with me, but I accepted a cup of tea and sat on a tree stump, trying to compose myself.

Then Guderian asked if I'm heading east, do I want to meet Russians?

"Of course not," I replied.

"Then you should keep to a side road and head west for Warsaw. The city is surrounded, but it is still held by the Poles."

I thanked him for his courtesy and we said good-bye. A short distance down the road, I passed a unit of German infantry. One soldier reached out to grab hold of me, just as I had turned to exchange a final wave of farewell with Guderian. That registered quickly with the soldier, as he let me continue on my way.

And so, that was my encounter with General Heinz Wilhelm Guderian. Much has been written about him after the war. On that September morning, you could sense he was a field commander on the hunt. He was slightly taller than I, just under six feet, and had not an unkindly face, square jaw and a suggestion of a smile as he talked. I could sense his men were in awe of him, and perhaps with good reason. We would not know until later that he was the commanding general of the XIX Corps, a part of the German Army Group North. I have attempted to reconstruct where my path crossed that of Guderian's corps. Bypassing Warsaw, two wings of his attack converged on their objective of Brzesc-Litewski, which they captured on September 17. Reversing from their southeasterly route, it seems likely that we met on September 14 or 15 near the town of Bielsk Podlaski, just south of the Narew River. Interestingly enough, the general would reappear in the life of a Rosinski, but that also comes later. We would learn that five years later Guderian left the stage of history, having been relieved of his position as chief of the general staff by Hitler, likely as a means of deflecting calls for him to negotiate a surrender to the allies.

My trip, now back south to Warsaw, would take at least 10 more days. As on the first leg north, I was able to survive, largely due to the hospitality of farmers and villagers along the way. There was no public transportation. Trains were no longer running, and bus service had been almost totally disrupted. On fortunate days, I was able to hitch a ride on a horse cart. Thank God for my school cap that earned both recognition and sympathy, and my boots, which had to be replaced halfway through my trek. The new pair, which I bought at a village shop with my meager savings, lasted me through all the war years. I slept in barns and under trees and when lucky enough, got a drink or handout of bread from a farmer's kitchen. On one day, I met a fisherman on the River Bug or a tributary and received a fat eel, which I took to a nearby farmhouse and managed to coax a pot

of eel soup from a kindly woman. Finally, on September 26, I reached Warsaw's eastern sector of Praga, crossed the Vistula River and headed for our apartment.

In the 23 days I had been gone, the landscape of Warsaw had changed dramatically. The destruction has been well documented, and for me it was overwhelming. Fortunately, our apartment building and surrounding buildings were not damaged, but other areas in the city center were completely destroyed. Still, to this day, the stench of dead rotting horses remains in my senses. German troop presence seemed to be surprisingly casual, as I was able to pass through the German cordon in the eastern sector of the city without difficulty. Some German patrols were

Jan's portrait, 1939.

stopping buses and street cars and ordering passengers out to the street so they could check personal documents. I learned later that one German attack route had passed through "Black Creek," the Rosinski family estate situated about 20 kilometers northeast of Warsaw. Their tracked vehicles tore up some of its land and crushed fences, but that was the only damage. The estate consisted mostly of forest and agricultural land. Within days, the manor house would be taken over as a headquarters and residence of a staff element of the German army. Staff cars and motorcycles could be seen coming and going, but there were no signs of troop elements, artillery or armor. My aunt Zofia Rosinska, the only family member then at the estate, did what she could to protest the requisition, but she was no match for the enemy.

My first stop was at Slawomir's house for the unpleasant task of informing the family of my lost contact with my cousin. Naturally, they were shocked and upset. This proved quite unpleasant, as this had become a second home to me. Their house was close to my institute and I often went there to take lunch and study. From there, I walked home to meet my mother, who by this time had become totally hysterical. She had been safe in the basement of the apartment during the bombings, and there were no losses. There was enough strength left in my legs that I decided to meet my closest friend and classmate, Jerzy Czechowicz. He had also received an induction order, but had not been able to get out of the city. He had been wounded, but, fortunately, not seriously. We took the occasion to celebrate that we both were still alive. Back in his apartment, Jerzy had a fine idea: "Let's open something special!" He reached into a cabinet and brought out a rare bottle of "mead," a classical Polish drink of fermented honey, bottled in 1776. The significance of the date did not escape us. After drinking less than half a glass, I immediately fell asleep. Later, still emboldened by this fine liquor, we decided to hit the streets, bottle in hand.

I had my own medical situation that needed to be taken care of. Walking into the city, I had been hit, apparently by a bullet fragment ricocheting off a wall. The wound was in my armpit but it was not serious and not bleeding much. I had the perfect surgeon in mind to take care of me, so Jerzy and I headed for a nearby hospital so I could be attended to by Dr. Zbyszka Sikorska. I was totally infatuated with her, but all my advances had proven futile. On this occasion she was stubborn as ever. We argued over how to remove the bullet fragment and after I had gently pushed her aside, she hit me with a roundhouse punch to the head and I was out for the duration of the brief operation. When I woke up, she was

Jan, Warsaw, 1935.

Jan (right) with a WIT classmate, Stefan Kisielewski, 1938.

sitting on top of me, having just finished the extraction. Adding insult to injury, I had been the butt of jokes on how I could have been wounded in such a place. It was suggested that I must have been in the act of surrendering, with my hands up. "How else could it have happened?" was their probing question.

Later, Dr. Zbyszka Sikorska, Dr. Barbara Natorff-Tokarczyk, her assistant surgeon (and my future wife), Jerzy, and two others were standing and chatting in front of the hospital. We were attracted by a nearby gathering of local residents and a German army colonel and a few armed soldiers. As we looked closer, the colonel had some boxes of canned food he was handing out to some local residents. I took a tin of some meat, and became intrigued with the self-opening device attached to it. The contents were quite good, and I could not resist commenting to the officer that this advanced can opener technology is an example why the Wehrmacht eventually will lose the war to the Americans and their ingenuity. I don't think it provoked much more of an answer than "we'll have to see." At least I wasn't arrested for my brashness. There were such times or incidents that showed the occupiers as sometimes benign. If they had been Russians, we all would have been captured and disposed of one way or another.

I ended the day by returning to my aunt Zofia Giedroyc's house near the institute for a long sleep. The next day would begin our scheming with friends and classmates that would lead to some of us joining the resistance. But first, to Russia, where I began my life.

CHAPTER 2

Family

Before descending into the wartime underground, it might be worthwhile to offer a short introduction to my family, starting in pre-revolutionary czarist Russia. Family records have long since vanished, so what is set herein is from my best recollections, drawn from stories my mother passed on to me. My father, Cezarjusz Rosinski, a Polish national, was an academic, having received his doctorate in chemistry from the Warsaw Institute of Technology, circa 1907. He was employed for a time by the Eiger concern to help oversee the building of the Wysoka Portland Cement plant in central Poland, which, I'm told, still exists today. The Eigers were a wealthy Jewish merchant family, and my father undoubtedly could have had a prosperous career with them, had he chosen to remain in Poland.

Having married my mother, Stanislawa Janina Jedynska, and following the first decade of the twentieth century, he began to harbor grave concerns about raising a family in a Poland that could be swept up yet again in conflicts arising from the tripartite partition of the former Polish-Lithuanian Commonwealth by Russia, Austria and Prussia. He could not have foreseen the outbreak of World War I in 1914, but he likely did sense the rising international tensions that impacted traditional Polish lands and heard the rumblings of war talk in Europe.

Such misgivings prompted him in 1915 to accept a position as a professor of chemistry at the principal university in Nizhny Novgorod, about 350 kilometers west of Moscow. It was renamed Gorky after the October Revolution of 1917, and then returned to its original name under the Russian Federation. I was born there on February 10, 1917, the month of the February Revolution and, with the abdication of Czar Nicholas II, the end of the Romanov dynasty. The nine-month civil war that followed soon penetrated the academic stability of the university. It was a time of character assassinations and purges. As an outsider, Professor Rosinski became a convenient target. Not only was he an outsider, he was an aristocrat as well, which reflected his Polish family's background. He also was a teetotaler, and this didn't seem to sit well with the often besotted leadership of the proletariat. He was arrested several times for anti–Socialist attitudes by local revolutionary activists and, at one point, he and my mother were evicted from their quarters at the university. Tragically, a prolonged sickness overtook him and he died of typhus at the age of 33 on March 29, 1920. The only memento I have of my father during those years in Russia is a letter he wrote to his parents in Warsaw, dated February 11, 1919, expressing worry that they were having difficulty finding milk for me, and describing the deteriorating living conditions. He wrote: "Life is getting worse and worse. It is especially difficult to feed baby 'Janek' because of rationing. He is still in good health, with a good appetite, even with black bread and potatoes, which is our staple diet. We have little protein, but have found horsemeat to be somewhat tasty, marinated in vinegar, creating a taste like brown hare. Now even this has disappeared. Lack of cold weather clothes and boots are also a problem. I have no energy for scientific work. We are spending most of these days just searching for food, and waiting in lines for Soviet-regulated portions of food. We hope to survive the cold, hunger and typhus. Wishing to see you all soon."

As my mother told me years later, there was nothing to decide: we had to return to Poland. She bundled me up, took bare essentials, boarded a train for Moscow, and transferred there to Warsaw. It must have been a harrowing experience, lasting weeks rather than days due to the havoc wrought by the last battles of the Russo-Polish War of 1919–1920. In our trek west toward Warsaw, she must have had to negotiate passage between attacking or retreating armies. She described the sometimes standing room only, given the press of passengers on the train, and, most of all, the drunkenness of soldiers, minor officials and assorted scoundrels. Many were carrying arms, making the journey all the more perilous. No food was available on the trains, so she carefully paid what money she had for small food items and hot tea at stations along the way. The only incident we had I caused myself. At one station stop, I had run along the platform and into a barbed wire fence, cutting my eye lid. I was patched up, but the scar remains as evidence of this journey.

Before reaching Warsaw, she related to me, she endured the frightening experience of being detained at a Soviet Army checkpoint. She was ordered to show her identity papers and mine as well. While her papers showed her Polish nationality, mine was a birth certificate revealing my birth in Nizhny Novgorod, and thus establishing my Russian identity. The officer in charge threatened to block our passage and also claimed it within his rights to keep me in the grasp of Mother Russia. My mother told the officer they would have to kill her before she would allow her baby to be taken from her. Tears flowed, and voices were raised. Finally, it appeared that the officer realized this was becoming more trouble than it was worth and he let us pass. Fortunately for Poland, a few days later, as Soviet forces threatened Warsaw, Marshal Pilsudski, the Polish Army commander, led a counterattack on April 13, 1920, and forced the withdrawal of the Russians from the country. Pilsudski's victory would soon be called "The Miracle at the River Wisla." Little did we know then that the Soviet Union would remember this military disgrace and exact revenge nearly 20 years later.

Arriving in Warsaw, my mother decided to accept the hospitality of her sister, Zofia Giedroyc, and mother of Slawomir and Leszek. My three uncles, Jozef, Stanislaw and Jan, soon called on my mother and, rather than offering, pointedly told her that they, the Rosinski family, would take charge of my upbringing. Her response, as she later laughingly told me, was direct and forceful: "You can go to hell!" And it was delivered in English. I should point out that both the Rosinski and Jedynski families were well educated and tutored in foreign languages. The Jedynski family, I might note, was associated with the Korab clan and coat of arms, claiming the noble motto *Deo Gloria* (Glory to God). My mother was raised speaking both French and Polish. French I could never master, so my linguistic efforts centered on German and English. Both would become important in my life, with German obviously the most critical in my school years and the underground life to come.

Despite my humble beginnings in Russia, we were a privileged Polish family, and a privileged education was the underpinning of the intelligentsia. I attended Wojciech Gorski

Jan's mother, Stanislawa Janina Rosinski, 1919.

Gymnasium, the premier preparatory school in Poland, graduating with honors in 1935. After one month of relaxing and skiing in the Tatra Mountains, it was time to move on to university. I elected to follow my father as a student at the Warsaw Institute of Technology (WIT). I had no particular interest in chemistry, but I was influenced in this direction by one of my father's former professors. The entrance examinations were highly competitive, drawing as many as 5,000 student applicants. I felt I did well enough on the exams, but admission came from another direction. The president of WIT telephoned my mother to ask whether I was related to Professor Rosinski, my father. When she confirmed that I was, he explained that each year he was granted the right to nominate one student directly to the institute, without examination. He then selected me for his nomination. While thankful for a guaranteed admission, I felt a sense of guilt for some time that I was depriving a deserving student of the appointment, when I did not need it. In any event, my university student life began, along with a lifelong passion for study, research and scientific challenges. New friendships and plans for the future were formed. Some of those friendships would carry on into the war years to come and even into the underground movement. Classmates and competitors such as Janusz Ciborowski and Adam Orzechowski were at the center of my circle of

friends. There were few girls at the institute, but most of those few were in the chemistry department. Natalia "Nata" Leszczynska, who was engaged to Slawomir Poroski, would soon show uncommon bravery in the underground. Wanda Fejgin was the only Jewish girl in the department, and we would cross paths later in the German-occupied streets of Warsaw.

Ewa Krasinska was also in the department and a good friend. In 1938, I was offered and accepted a position as assistant to Professor Struszynski in the laboratory of the Department of Chemical Analysis, and held that position until the outbreak of the war a year later.

Jan's father, Cezarjusz Rosinski, 1919.

My mother's determination to raise me as she saw fit did not falter, as she sought some way to be self-supporting. Calculating correctly that my father had established his professional credentials with the business group owned by the Eiger family, she approached them, asking for employment. Her strategy worked, as she was offered an office position at a central office. She then had sufficient income to rent an apartment and pay for my early schooling. I don't know whether guilt finally got the best of my uncles, but over a period of time they eventually reached an accommodation with my mother and became active in my life and upbringing. Three of them were independent financially and were generous in supporting me, and probably my mother as well.

Jan was the oldest of the three, and would have been about 47 years old when World War II broke out. From 1913, as a recruit, he served in IX Regiment of Field Artillery in the Russian Army, until 1918, to the end of World War I. He was not physically imposing, at five feet, seven inches, but stocky and extremely strong. Jan was also an expert horseman. I recall an exciting day with him at a circus that had come to the city. The center ring in the big tent featured a trick horseman, displaying various riding positions while the horse circled the ring. Jan criticized his amateurishness, then suddenly leaped over the barrier and sought out the circus director. He convinced the man he could show a more credible performance, and got the green light to mount the

Jan's mother with 2-year-old Jan in Nizhniy Novgorod, Russia, 1919.

lead horse. Jan's performance was greeted with a standing ovation from the crowd.

Jan was a graduate of the Business College of the Council of Businessmen of Warsaw. Following college, from 1926 to 1940, he became the head bookkeeper in Eiger-owned Wysoka Group of Portland Cement plants near the city of Lublin. He never married, but as I recall, he didn't deny himself the enjoyment of life. I believe his devotion to his mother and two youngest sisters, Zofia and Stefania, distracted him from other social pursuits. There was one very nice woman, who was related to a long-deceased Polish king, but she apparently spurned any serious advances from him. Jan lived in a manor house and was chauffeured in a large sedan. On frequent occasion, he would send the car to pick me up in the morning and deliver me to school. He took a commission as a captain, or perhaps a higher rank, in the army at the outset of the war and saw heavy combat.

I recall that in the summer of 1935, Uncle Jan and I had what may have been an early glimpse of the German army, or at least German officers, who invaded Poland four years later. The German shooting team selected for the 1936 Olympics was on tour in Poland, and Jan had invited them to our family's Black Creek estate for an exhibition match with Polish marksmen. I was included in the latter as I had established a competitive place in the prospective Polish team, even at the age of 17. There was some suspicion that the Germans were all army officers, assigned not only to display their marksmanship, but to also observe places and people while in Poland, especially the Polish military.

In the pistol competition that day, I had fired three rounds, all in the bull's-eye. I had expected to be given a "100" score, but received only a "90." I must have been too much to bear for our visitors, as I told them, "I do not shoot 90's, only 100's." The Germans argued the score, so I requested an examination of the target. It was retrieved by a pulley mechanism to the firing line, and we all gathered around to prove our respective scoring. Using a magnifying glass, our guests reluctantly agreed that at least two shots had not missed the target, but actually entered the same bullet hole as my first shot. Unfortunately, I missed being selected for the Olympic team by one man, but I was pleased that one of our team marksmen won the pistol competition.

Misfortune fell on Jan soon after the invasion, when the Eiger businesses were closed. The Eiger family fled to Switzerland and left no one behind to manage their factories. Later, from 1940 to 1944, Uncle Jan was able to take a position as manager or director of a major private estate owned by a Polish nobleman, Count Adam Branicki. One incident involv-

Jan Rosinski walking with a WIT classmate, Danuta Chylinska.

ing Branicki has stayed in my mind. When a Polish man openly criticized the performance of the armed forces in defending the country against the Germans, Graf Branicki challenged him to a duel. German commanders in the area of the estate looked on this as a sporting event and supplied dueling pistols, as well as supervision of the dueling protocol. Branicki was lucky. His dueling opponent missed his shot, while Branicki's merely winged the man's ear. The incident ended with claimed satisfaction on both sides. However, with me there remained a sensitive issue with Branicki. He sought to enlist Uncle Jan's support for a future marriage commitment between me and his daughter. We deflected his approaches on several occasions, and I was finally able extricate myself from this awkward situation.

Uncle Stanislaw was the youngest of the three, tall, lanky, blond and energetic. He was also educated in business, just as were his brothers Jan and Jozef; he was an alumni of the same business college. He was blessed with a beautiful and loving wife, Halina, who always welcomed me to their home. Unfortunately, they never had children, so perhaps I filled that role, at least in her eyes. Stanislaw amassed financial wealth through various business dealings, including the sale of forest lands, either as owner or agent. The same as Jan, he worked in Branicki's private estate, having a part in its administration. In his private life, he was a very close friend of Count Adam Branicki and was living in a house belonging to the count. He took a commission in the army prior to the invasion, and made a name for himself in a series of engagements along the German invasion route. I knew that he was highly decorated, but he rarely, if ever spoke of his exploits. Amazingly, he was captured on at least four occasions and, with

the exception of the last capture, he was rescued by his men. After the last capture, he was brought before General Guderian, who had to decide what to do with him. Perhaps because of Stanislaw's bravery or some other personal attribute, Guderian offered him parole if Stanislaw would give his guarantee that he would not take up arms again. This meeting with Guderian did come after the Polish armed forces had officially surrendered to the German command in Warsaw. Stanislaw saw the handwriting on the wall and retired to civilian life in Warsaw. He returned home ill with pneumonia and tuber-

Uncle Jozef Rosinski as an army officer during the border war with Lithuania in 1919.

Jan (left) and his uncle Jan Rosinski, Tatra Mountains, 1938.

culosis, from which he ultimately died at the age of 44, in 1942, in the special tuberculosis hospital in Otwock, where he was treated for the last two years of his life. I sometimes wondered whether General Guderian might have remembered my name from our roadside encounter, and associated it with Stanislaw. However, the general likely had more on his mind than making such a correction.

I recall that Stanislaw harbored hatred for Russians. To my knowledge, this did not grow out of any particular incident or experience; he simply hated Russians for being Russian. Most of us in our extended family could speak German, so we could communicate with them, but not Russians, and certainly not in their language which none of us studied or understood.

My Uncle Jozef was close to Jan's age and also a graduate from Business College of the Council of Businessmen of Warsaw, and later was studying at the Political Science College, in the Department of Finances

Stefan Kawecki, Jan, and his uncle Jan (left to right), Tatra Mountains, 1938.

and Economy, in Warsaw. He was on active duty as a junior army officer 1919–1920 during the border war with Lithuania; also he was well known for the Sejny Uprising in 1919, a region presently in the northeastern part of Poland. He was awarded the Cross of Independence by the President of the Republic of Poland in 1931. A photograph of Jozef with fellow officers is among the few taken of the family. Jozef was the anglophile of the family, having spoken English at home from childhood. This undoubtedly earned him his position as a head of the Polish branch of Burroughs Office Machines, an American corporation. He also worked for some time in the Kodak Company's office in Poland. In addition, his ties to England likely included cooperation with external British intelligence (MI6) before the war. I recall learning inadvertently that he was awarded a medal for his service. Years later, when staying temporarily in London, I visited MI6 and had the audacity to inquire about Jozef's possible service to the Crown. After initial obfuscation by MI6, I was given a bureaucratic non-reply and escorted to the door. Thus, my uncle's service shall rest in peace.

The most important person in my life throughout the time of resistance, an escape from a prisoner of war camp in Germany to an allied occupation zone, and finally as an émigré to America was my future wife, Barbara (nee Natorff-Tokarczyk) Rosinski. Barbara was born in Warsaw in 1922. Her father was a very wealthy industrialist entrepreneur, but one who, unfortunately, gave more time to intimacies outside the family than within. As a result, Barbara chose to leave home while a university student, concentrating on her studies as a medical student at the Warsaw University. She became an accomplished surgeon, serving later in both the Polish Army and in the AK underground. Her story and life continue with mine.

CHAPTER 3

The Underground

I was in a state of shock with the surrender of Polish forces on September 27, the day after returning from my "eastern adventure," and failure, I might add, to join the army. Little good it would have done, given Poland's capitulation before September was out. I met with some of my professors, but classes at the WIT were now impossible, with the closure of all schools by edict of the occupation. I had yet to complete my thesis for graduation and that was prominent on my mind. In any event, the institute had not escaped considerable damage from aerial bombing and artillery fire during the siege. We students gathered in small numbers to discuss what we could do under these circumstances. Undoubtedly, it was in these hidden meetings that thoughts of conspiracy first arose. However, it would be conspiracy of the individual, as each of us sought some way to make a mark against the Third Reich.

Soon after my return to Warsaw, I met with my uncle Stanislaw and told him of my encounter with General Guderian. This was when I learned of Stanislaw's capture. When I asked why he was not in a POW camp, he replied that "theoretically" he was. Stanislaw then explained he had been offered, and accepted, parole from active military service. Of course, the Polish surrender came soon thereafter, but he most assuredly had been spared languishing indefinitely in a camp as a prisoner. A parole was almost an unheard of act in those times, and could only have been given by a very high command authority. I cannot recall Stanislaw acknowledging Guderian as the authority, but I concluded it had to have been so. This was yet another human courtesy extended by an unusual gentleman general.

In the aftermath of the Polish surrender, the German commanders in Warsaw laid out security plans for a victory parade through the city center. Nothing could have been more provocative to the Polish people than such a display of military presence — and deserving of special attention by the resistance in its early stages of forming. On October 5, 1939, Hitler made his only visit to Warsaw. Standing on a podium, he reviewed the passing troops of the German 8th Army. Underneath the podium, a high-explosive bomb had been planted that would have removed the Fuehrer and the top army command, as well as Joseph Goebbels, from history. Any explanation for what occurred remains obscured. However, at the last minute an order apparently was issued that the bomb was to be removed or defused and the team involved ordered to move to a new location for some other operation. Hitler departed Warsaw later that afternoon, unaware of how close he had come to being killed. Fortune would be with him again four years later when he narrowly missed assassination in the Stauffenberg incident at the command conference in the Wolf's Lair, next to the town of Ketrzyn, in Poland. How history might have turned dramatically on either event, but certainly more so in that early war year of 1939.

In the meantime, while coming to a decision about what to do with my life, I was approached by Professor Slawinski, a member of the WIT faculty and also a member of a very wealthy entrepreneurial family. He felt a deep sense of compassion for the institute's students, who had been displaced by the destruction in the city. He offered his family's manor house, located near the Tomb of the Unknown Soldier in the city center as a temporary hostel. He also arranged for some basic food supplies and asked that I oversee the entire effort. He then gave me the keys to what really was a palace. I wanted to refuse, but under the circumstances, I could not. He knew that I would be fair and honest in looking after the residence, and especially in seeing that the female students would not face any difficulties. Beyond this, he apparently also entrusted me with the safe-keeping of the family's well-stocked wine cellar. In fact, I did keep it locked and off limits.

I also was involved in a business endeavor for a few weeks when a friend from the institute asked me to join him in replacing broken windows in the apartments and houses in our neighborhood. He had purchased a supply of glass, window frames and a small cart, which was all that was needed to operate a very profitable enterprise in very high demand. In many areas of the city there didn't seem to be one window undamaged. This was a constructive diversion, but my mind kept turning to ways of creating problems for our occupiers. Drawing on my chemistry skills, I may have launched one of the first clandestine operations against the vaunted *Wehrmacht*. Together with my friend and chemistry department classmate Natalia "Nata" Leszczynska, we put together a plan to make the

German army's consumption of beer an unpleasant experience, or at least for one encampment in Warsaw. Rummaging through the chemistry department at my institute, I found a supply of uranium salts in the laboratory, as well as a small amount of alkaloids and a kilo of morphine. We were then able to recruit two Polish boys who worked as waiters in the German officers club to pour some of these "ingredients" into kegs of beer. Fortunately, the color of the chemicals was close to that of beer. Nata asked me what effect this would have. I could only reply, "I haven't the faintest idea. It has radioactive properties, so maybe they'll glow." Nata laughed as she pictured a "glowing army of the night." It likely did not create much damage or poisoning, but we did not hang around to find out. Thus, the results of this first modest operation remained an unknown to us.

After Christmas and the New Year, however, it was time to make some serious decisions. Without consulting anyone in my family or any of my friends, I decided to commit myself to service with the underground Home Army, or *Armia Krajowa* (AK). As it turned out, Wlodzimierz Krynicki, a classmate of mine, had recommended, or nominated, me to the AK. I requested that I be inducted on my birthday, February 10, 1940. Krynicki came to our apartment with two AK recruiters, whom my mother thought to be murderers or gangsters, at least in appearance. After answering several questions regarding my background, I swore allegiance on the Bible and selected my code name as "Halszka," a woman's name to confuse the enemy and also that of my first cousin. I was told that I would be contacted again in a few days for further instructions. Two AK officers, including one woman, did meet with me briefly to discuss security procedures and meeting arrangements, but no duties were yet assigned. The woman never appeared again, and when I asked about her, I was told she was killed in an operation in Krakow.

Much has been written about the many-tiered organization of the Polish underground. The exile government was headquartered in London. At the head of government was the president, as a supreme commander, followed by the premier, the National Council of Ministers and the Ministry of Internal Affairs. Subordinate to that office was the Delegatura of two persons, one in Poznan in the territory annexed by Germany and the other with the "General Government" in Warsaw; then there were 13 different departments equivalent to the prewar ministries. Military organization and commands were not formalized until the Home Army was established in mid–February 1942. Thus, my induction came two years ahead of the formalities for the AK itself.

The underground took an earlier form in the aftermath of the September 28–29 capitulation as the Polish Victory Service (SZP), and soon thereafter as the Union for Armed Struggle (ZWZ). Both were subordinate to the exile government leadership. However, these organizations and reorganizations mattered little to those of us at the street level. Our focus, first and foremost, was on daily survival, and then to collecting our resources to fight the occupiers. It was on the streets of Warsaw and other cities that the underground moved among the people. Our presence and activities gave a psychological lift to the citizenry and, in turn, we drew moral and spiritual sustenance from them. I can recall no instance during the entire years of occupation, when confronted with imminent danger, that I was denied help or refuge when most needed. There was also a special camaraderie among university students, who had been shut out from pursuing their education and professional lives. Their many talents and determination would now be felt in different ways.

For the duration of the occupation, or actually until I and a few others were transported in 1944 to a POW camp in Germany, no one in our family ever spoke about what each of us was doing, or may have been doing, in a secret life. We were all engaged, possibly including my mother, in some form of clandestine activity. We all followed the simple rule: "What you don't know, you can't tell." Reports leaked out early on about the vicious methods of torture employed by the Gestapo and other German security elements. When I asked my friend Dr. Zbyszka Sikorska what she had heard about German torture methods or people she may have treated as a result of them, she said the most common methods were injections or so-called truth serums, electric shock, and hot probes to the body or under fingernails. I took the foolish step of testing myself as to my level of resistance. I heated some nails over coals in our apartment stove until they were white hot and pushed one or two into my thigh. While I was able to stave off screaming, I nearly passed out. The stench was overwhelming, which greatly upset my mother when she came home. To calm her down, I explained that I had accidentally brushed up against the stove and got burned. Later that afternoon, I went to the hospital where Zbyszka worked to have the wounds treated. She said they looked like self-inflicted wounds, which I couldn't deny. She admonished me, but bandaged the wounds, which healed cleanly. Both Zbyszka and Barbara, my future wife, were medical officers and surgeons in the Home Army, and served with great skill and sacrifice. Wisely, I stopped testing my resistance to possible methods of interrogation and torture.

Through a very unusual series of events, I developed a hope that I could contribute a unique skill to the AK. Some may have thought it to be a phenomenon of the supernatural or foretelling the future. In reality, it was neither, but I'll let what I experienced speak for itself. About a month or so before the German invasion, I was studying at home for a chemistry examination. Quite suddenly, I was able to see in my mind's eye a list of equations and questions which looked to represent a test or examination — perhaps the one I would face the next day. I was able to solve all the problems on the list, except for the last equation, on which I simply had a mental block. I hurriedly wrote down all that I was able to recognize and, with Nata, took the paper with me the next day to the examination room. Nata was as astounded as I when there on the blackboard were the exact same equations and questions that I had written down the previous day. I finished the exam, with the exception of the last problem, which again totally perplexed me. Professor Leja, who was monitoring the examination, and who later would become the head of the mathematics department at Cambridge University, challenged me to complete this last problem: "Why don't you take your time, you should be able to finish this final problem — it's a simple transformation." I acknowledged he was right, but I could not explain the difficulty I was having. So, I said, "Please, let's forget about it. I'll just have to accept a 'B' rather than an 'A.'" After the examination, I also confided in Professor Edward Rossenberg my experience. He and his wife had moved to Warsaw from Vienna, where he was on the faculty of the major university there. As he was a Jew, perhaps it would be more accurate to say that they had fled Vienna after Germany's annexation of Austria — the *Anschluss*— in March 1938.

Then a second "incident" occurred in a more convoluted manner during the winter of 1939. What occurred then was not related to the underground, but a social diversion away from those daily risks. My close friend Stefan Kawecki and I were on a skiing trip in the Tatra Mountains with a girlfriend, a Polish resident of Switzerland, about whom I began having serious intentions. After three days of skiing, Stefan and I decided to go on a longer trek to an area known as the "Gooseneck." We would be leaving my friend behind, she to return to Switzerland. I asked if she would write a postcard in my name to my first cousin Halszka as a family courtesy and to tell her of our delayed plans to return to Warsaw. When my friend asked how she could write it in my name when Halszka could plainly see it was not my handwriting. I told her it didn't matter as she has never seen my handwriting, and that she simply would be happy to hear from me. My friend agreed to send the postcard, and we parted company. The next five days in the mountains turned into a harrowing experience for both Stefan and me. Unexpected new snowfalls impeded our cross-country skiing and led to our exhaustion and near physical collapse. We finally made it back to civilization after a forced ski march of sorts to the resort at Zakopane, and then back to Warsaw by bus. I should note that these annual trips to the Tatras were not just for frivolous vacations. Stefan, a civil engineering student at WIT, and I found this to be a useful diversion to recharge our batteries and become mentally prepared for the school term to come and examinations.

After our return to Warsaw, I received phone calls from several friends about a big dinner party Halszka was hosting, which apparently had something to do with me. Since this was news to me, as our apartments were within walking distance from each other I decided to visit her and solve the mystery myself. There was no one at home except the maid, so I asked her about the dinner. She explained that Halszka was so happy to receive the 14 intimate letters I had sent that she wanted to have this party. I was stunned, of course, realizing a greater mystery needed to be solved. I could only conclude that Halszka had simply lost her mind. On the appointed evening, I asked Nata and Zbyszka Sikorska to come with me to Halszka's apartment early, to see if we could look into the matter of these letters. Their feminine curiosities were sufficiently piqued so that it was not difficult to recruit their help. We were the first guests to arrive. Halszka was still dressing, so we had a few moments of privacy to investigate. The maid pointed out the letters wrapped in blue ribbon on a silver dish in the dining room. We were able to open two of the letters. Zbyszka was quick to see that the intimate prose and style was the handwriting of a woman and that it was meant for me — that my friend was using this as a medium to attract my attention. How strange!

Well, this now turns into another side story. Zbyszka, who had once been the subject of my honorable attentions, and to whom I actually had proposed marriage, immediately launched her anger: "I will not forget this ever! How could you possibly be interested in entertaining another girl, when you are interested in me?" I reminded her that she had long since spurned my proposals and claimed that she never intended to marry. Collecting myself, I said, "Look, let's just get out of this somehow. I cannot tell Halszka I didn't write those letters, it will become a scandal. Let's join the dinner and somehow survive tonight, or let me survive it."

During dinner, Nata sat across from me, and sometime during the main course of the meal, she drew everyone's attention by announcing she had a dream about me the previous night "in color" and proceeded to tell all. I interrupted her story, and said, "Let me finish it for you." When I did so, Nata was clearly shaken: "How could you know this? I've told no one!" "I don't know," I replied, "but I had the same dream." Later, over coffee, Professor Rossenberg, who was also invited, came to me and said, "You know, Jan, you must nurse this thing, this ability you have and put it to good use." Still stupefied myself, I asked him, "Well, how can I nurse something I don't know I have, or don't know anything about?" Thus ended for the time being any discussion of this unexplained phenomenon. After the dinner party, I arranged for a horse carriage to take Zbyszka home. She took the opportunity to light into me again about my pursuit of another woman — that I had done a horrible thing by not telling her. Defending myself, reminding her of my multiple proposals and her multiple refusals, finally I said, "Well, you didn't want me, so what do you expect from me for heavens sake?" Then, passing a small park, the driver told us, "I'm stopping the carriage here and going over there and sit on that park bench. When you're through arguing, I'll come back and drive you home." Ten minutes later, we were on our way again. Despite a rather disagreeable end to the evening, the unanswered questions about my experiences remained hanging in my mental background, and perhaps acted as a subtle catalyst in my joining the AK.

The final and last occurrence of the phenomenon came on May 9, 1940. While at home, my studying was interrupted by images coming clear in my mind of a massive attack of German forces against Holland and Belgium. I was able to focus on bomber attacks on airfields in both countries, as well as the extensive use of paratroopers dropped into strategic points in Holland. I also focused on mechanized movements, but this was less clear. I had already informed higher AK echelons of my unusual experiences, which were met with expected skepticism. Nevertheless, I could only call them again to report what I had observed in my mind's eye. They told me they would investigate and call me back. They did just that, and I was told they had heard nothing, either from London or on the BBC. The next morning, May 10, the German army and air force launched a multi-pronged attack against these two countries. As was the case against Poland, the Luftwaffe led with strategic bombing of airfields, along with confirmed reports of significant deployments of paratroops behind Dutch defensive lines. My senior AK contact called me: "Well, Jan, you were right. However, what did you really see?" Thinking further, I told him my sense was that somehow I intercepted the plans or preparation of the plans or orders that were drawn up for what Hitler had labeled "Felsennest," or "Rocky Nest" (Skalne Gniazdo). What I now recall is that I did not "pick up" on General Guderian's role in again leading the XIX Panzer Corps through Luxembourg, on through the Ardennes, the capture of Liege, and to just short of Dunkirk. In the aftermath of my report, I was asked or encouraged to do what I could to trigger what they now reluctantly recognized as my unusual capabilities. Their suggestions included placing myself in the proximity or company of German officers in order to intercept their conversations and even their unexpressed thoughts or operational planning.

All of this was intriguing, but I didn't want it to become a distraction from carrying out my activities in the underground. A first priority was to establish a viable cover for my travels throughout Warsaw and occasionally outside the city. Nearly three years earlier, in 1936, as the treasurer of the WIT student union, I learned of my possible forgery talent. It was the Christmas season and I had purchased some small gifts for my student friends and signed a check. At the cashier stand in the bookstore, I was invited to the manager's office and told that I was suspected of a forged signature on the check I had just signed. To verify my actual signature on file, the manager had me sign my name 50 times. He and I discovered that each signature was different, even by a small degree. My check was finally accepted, along with the manager's comment that I had the "talent" of becoming the perfect forger.

So, with the occupation upon us, I set out to re-create myself. We were able to acquire samples of basic German documents, and I then created my own ID card, or *Ausweis*, as well as an authorization order as an approved supplier of agricultural and animal products for the German occupation forces. Further, I was able to arrange for authentication, or backstopping, of the documents at a German document control office should anyone make inquiries. To protect myself further, I needed to conduct my daily activities in a manner that would support who and what my papers said I was. This was especially important during the harvest season, which should be my busiest time. Come winter, I could relax more, or not stay fixed to a rigid work schedule.

The fear that I had when stopped by German soldiers for a document inspection never abated. Fortunately the forms I used were genuine, with copies filed with an occupation logistics office for agricultural production and supply. Then came the day when I failed to pass German scrutiny. I was skiing in the Tatra Mountains and in a lift area when a young officer came up to me as I was carrying my skis to the lift. He asked for my papers just as I had a very timely epiphany. Still examining them carefully, I asked whether he was Jennewein, who won a gold medal and two silver medals in the 1939 World Skiing Championships in Zakopane, Poland. He seemed surprised and smiled, but his smile did not hide a sharp suspicious gaze straight into my eyes. I broke out in a cold sweat, as it was clear we

exchanged silent acknowledgment that my papers were for-
geries. Yet, he backed away and
let me pass. As I nodded my
understanding of his surpris-
ing leniency, he again came
up to me, put his hand on my
arm and led me through a
cordon of gestapo men. A
few days later, I was suddenly
trapped in the ski lift's gondola headed to the top of the
Kasprowy Wierch peak. To
my horror, I realized that I
was surrounded by a group of
high-ranking SS and Gestapo
officers. They were watching
me intensely as if I was a
criminal or spy. There was no
way to escape. At the peak,
one of the SS officers asked

Jan in Tatra Mountains, Poland, 1938.

me, "Who are you and what are you doing here?" Scared to death by the
thought that I would be killed or executed, I couldn't manage an answer.
Miraculously I spotted Jennewein, who appeared ready to greet these
officers already interrogating me inside the gondola. He quickly approached
me, put his hand on my shoulder, and announced "He is my friend, don't
trouble yourselves." He then walked me through the gathering of officers
to freedom. Before he let me go, he leaned close to me, and quietly said,
"For God's sake, ski out of here and don't come back!" And I did just that.

Over a year later, I read a report in the Nazi newspaper *Völkischer
Beobachter* of his death in 1943 on the Eastern Front in Russia. I could
not help but be emotionally distressed at this news. He had, in fact, saved
my life, especially if I had fallen into the hands of the Gestapo. According
to the news report, he was born in 1919, two years after me. Many years
later I learned that Josef "Pepi" Jennewein was born at St. Anton in the
Tyrolean Alps, Austria, on November 21, 1919, and served as a Luftwaffe
fighter pilot, with 86 reported "kills." He went missing in 1943 behind
Red Army lines. The fact that he was Austrian, rather than German, might
be the clue to why he treated me with such courtesy, or perhaps barely
disguised sympathy.

Later during the winter, and after my encounter with Jennewein, I crossed paths with other Austrians in the Tatra Mountains. I was on a ski outing with three other classmates and a professor when we were nearly trapped in a heavy snowfall. We sought overnight shelter in an unoccupied hut. Our attention was immediately drawn to a warning on the wall, stating that the Gestapo would be coming through the area at 11:00 in the morning. We vacated the hut before the hour and hid behind some rocks a safe distance away. A car with Gestapo officers did arrive. They stopped long enough to inspect the hut and then drove off. We waited a half-hour for insurance and then returned to the hut for the night. We were eating at a picnic table in front of the hut in the early evening when three men wearing sporting clothes approached us. One of them asked if we had a flashlight they could borrow to search their hut for something they had lost. We had a flashlight, so we gave it to them. My friend said, "Well, that's the last we'll see of that flashlight." An hour or so later, one of the three returned the flashlight wrapped in paper. Back in the hut, I unwrapped it and found a note: "Tomorrow the Gestapo will come again at 11:00 A.M." It was signed "The Austrians." I don't believe this incident was connected in any way with Jennewein, but we could be thankful that at least some unknown Austrians were not totally enamored with their political overlords in the Third Reich.

In one of my earlier assignments, I served as a courier link in receiving and passing maps, German and Polish, to a higher command in the AK. However, the set times for passing them were often not met, thus risking the security of the operation. In one instance, my lengthy wait for contact at Warsaw's central train station drew the attention of Gestapo officers, who inspected my papers. I told them I was waiting to receive agricultural maps for the logistics office where I was assigned. This seemed to satisfy them, but not me. I registered my strong criticism of this lax performance to a senior AK officer. This was not the first time I shared my opinions with higher echelons, which likely labeled me as an outspoken and headstrong soldier.

Another similar incident soon occurred. I had waited much longer than I should have, well over an hour, for a courier contact at an electric train station in Warsaw. A man in civilian clothes approached me, displaying his Gestapo credentials. He told me he had observed me loitering on the platform while several trains arrived and departed. "What are you doing?" he demanded. I told him I was waiting for a woman friend who was often late. With a grim look on his face, he stepped closer, signaling that trouble was coming. Fortune, however, was with me that afternoon.

Just at that moment, a young woman with whom I was casually acquainted stepped onto the station platform. I exclaimed, "here she comes now!" and rushed over to her with an embrace and a kiss. Of course, she was stunned, but before she could react, I whispered, "Let's just get out of here and I'll explain later!" I did, once outside the station and out of the grasp of the Gestapo officer, who did not pursue further questioning. She relaxed and finally smiled as I thanked her for rescuing me. After walking some distance away from the station, we parted. I don't remember seeing her again. Yet here was another citizen playing a small but important role at a critical moment. My report on the incident and failed contact with the courier did not register with my higher command, such was their attention on more important matters.

Perhaps it was my natural irreverence for authority, or at least military authority, that eventually allowed me to operate within the AK somewhat independently. I think that sometimes the higher command simply didn't know what to do with me. Within my group of five or so conspirators, mostly all classmates or friends from my institute, we first set out to assign various tasks and cooperation with each other. I was selected to be the spy for the group because of some speaking ability in German and Russian. Initially, we used my apartment for meetings. Having a look at my fellow conspirators, my mother suggested I improve my class of associates, as they all looked to be criminals. I also arranged to hold some meetings at our Black Creek estate, despite the fact that there were Germans occupying the manor house and grounds. They recognized me as a member of the estate family, so they did not pay that much attention to me and my visiting friends. The lumber mill was not working, so there was no significant work activity going on. Thus, we were able to meet in privacy. We discussed the possibilities of conducting sniper attacks on selected targets and stringing wire across roads that saw frequent motorcycle traffic — one of the hated symbols of the invading army. Not much was accomplished, but I did attempt to string wire in two locations that had trees on both sides of the road. Either my timing was off or the risks in waiting so long for passing traffic eventually turned our attention to other activities.

One of my first tasks was to case, or observe, a restaurant in the city center frequented by German officers and soldiers. The objective of the exercise was to determine whether the restaurant should be targeted for a bomb attack at a peak hour. I recruited my friend Nata from WIT to sit with me on the curb across the street from the restaurant and eat pumpkin seeds. For each officer, we would throw a seed shell into one small bag and into another bag for each soldier. We did this for only two days, but someone had told my mother that I had been seen sitting in the gutter with an attractive girl, eating something. She was waiting for me when I came home on the second evening. "Have you lost your mind?" she demanded. Well, I had no defense, but I was told by the AK that my report on the traffic at the restaurant would be sent to the command in London to determine whether an operation would be organized. As it turned out, a decision was made not to go ahead with the bombing.

Before the year 1940 was out, I was tapped by the AK to help organize and conduct what we called a "pioneer course" in sabotage operations. This was undertaken under the aegis of the newly organized Union for Revenge (*Zwiazek Odwetu*). Nearly 20 men, one of several groups, were recruited for the training. This included use of chemical contaminants, road mining, planted bombs, and the like. To provide safety for such a large group, we set up the training outside Warsaw in a large forested area of Falenica near the town of Otwock. The men were armed primarily with nonmilitary weapons, hunting rifles and shotguns. For the two months of training, we holed up in the ruins of old World War I fortifications and tunnels, made safe due to the fact that the entire forest was off limits to German troops for fear of attacks by our resistance. As an extra measure of caution, however, we did not start cooking fires because of the danger that smells and smoke might attract unwanted attention. So, our daily fare was usually bread, cheese, and perhaps small amounts of cooked meat, if we could find any, and raw vegetables. After completing the training, all the men were dispersed to various AK commands. We did try one or two actual operations before disbanding. One was a successful effort to take out German motorcycle courier riders heading to Warsaw on the main highway from Otwock. At least twice we strung wire across the road from tree to tree just before daybreak and managed to instantly eliminate the forward motion of the rider and thus capture valuable documents in his pouch. The enemy would send out search patrols but would never enter the area where our fortifications were.

I was involved in one other training activity the following year for our version of chemical warfare. Following up my earlier efforts to contaminate a German beer supply, we looked to other ways to contaminate food and drink consumed by German soldiers. We recruited about ten AK members for a ten-week course and then sent them on to their respective assignments. Typical chemicals used were potassium cyanide, strong bacteria-based substances, morphine and various alkaloids. The training was given in a vacated house in the upscale area on Chlodna Street. We had to be extremely careful with this many men coming and going to the house. We staggered their arrivals and departures, and thus managed to avoid an informant's eyes or a German patrol. Our ability to move about was also greatly aided by the total patriotism and loyalty of the city's citizens to the AK. Neighbors and passersby knew by instinct what we were about so a wall of silence reigned.

To be the perfect spy, I realized, it was necessary to take the time to improve my German language skills. After a lengthy search for a teacher, I learned that Edward Rossenberg was available. I have mentioned him as a former professor at the University of Vienna. However, I knew him then as Edward Rzepecki, a Jew who together with his wife, Maria, had fled just before the *Anschluss*, the German annexation of Austria in 1938. After our initial meeting, he agreed to hold two sessions each week and said that he would accept food, such as potatoes and vegetables, in lieu of cash. Beyond his rigorous teaching skills, I soon gathered the impression there was more to Rzepecki than a professor-in-exile. Whether he was intentionally careless with me or not I didn't know, but I began to feel somewhat uneasy in his apartment. From time to time, I noticed what appeared to be unusual maps and drawings. I did not know at the time that he was Jewish, so that did not enter into my thinking. Nevertheless, my warning signals were flashing that something was amiss.

I decided to go to his apartment at least 30 minutes ahead of our lesson time for a month to observe the apartment from a stairwell across a central courtyard. My patience was rewarded after the third observation attempt. I stood up in absolute shock as I saw a man in the uniform of a Luftwaffe colonel hurriedly make his way to Rzepecki's apartment door and enter quickly. I threw caution to the wind and ran straight to the apartment. The colonel was still standing with his back to the door when Rzepecki opened it. Naturally surprised, Rzepecki blurted out, "All right Jan, you have found out. I am working with the British, so why don't you come in. We can study and also fight the Germans." Still stunned, I could only reply, "Well, don't tell me more. I will do what I can." Even uncomfortable as I was, Rzepecki invited me to stay and have tea. With the shock worn off, the colonel turned out to be a rather friendly fellow, having found amusement in this bizarre situation. He was a handsome man, and appeared young for his rank, no more than in his late 20s. We were introduced and shook hands. As I look back on the incident, it certainly wasn't the normal modus operandi for spies. The technical drawings I saw on a table must have been the subject of their meeting, but I asked no questions. I decided on the spot that I would not report this development to the AK. I then learned that my teacher had changed his name to Rapacki, but he later admitted that his true family name was Rossenberg. He told me that he and Maria had to flee Austria after he learned that Hitler had personally put him on a blacklist for assassination for writing "malicious propaganda" against the Third Reich. Gradually, I helped him when and where I could, primarily in forging documents that he needed for people he was helping to hide or disappear. Assuming Rossenberg did, in fact, work for British intelligence, or MI6, perhaps he might have mentioned my name in his secret communications with his contacts or minders. Thus, I've always wondered whether my name might be buried somewhere in MI6 files.

The Rossenbergs' life in Warsaw continued without incident or threats to their security, so Maria decided she wanted to take a vacation at the resort town of Zakopane in the Tatra Mountains. I don't recall whether she planned to go alone or with others, but Edward couldn't dissuade her from going. I told her she would be taking a foolish risk, given the considerable presence there of German soldiers on leave, not to mention the Gestapo, which seemed to be everywhere. I also invited her to stay at the family estate for a few days of relaxation, but that didn't seem to please her. She ignored my severe warnings and Edward's opposition, so off she went. She did agree to telephone or write a postcard when she reached Zakopane. However, after two or three days there was no news. Nothing. Edward was beside himself, so I needed to step into the situation. I contacted Witold Puc, a close friend and classmate at WIT: "Look, Witold, I know you are not a member of the AK, but I trust you just the same. I need to ask a favor." I explained the situation to him, and told him I could not go myself for security reasons. He accepted my urgent request that he travel to Zakopane and attempt to find out what had happened to Maria. I instructed him to contact Zosia Gasienica-Gladczan, an active member of the AK in Zakopane, for help. I told Witold that the absence of any news did not bode well for positive news. I further explained that, in the worst case, the answer might be found in a grave. Nevertheless, we needed to make every effort to confirm that either Maria was still alive or had been killed after her capture. Zosia was aware of an area in a local cemetery in Zakopane where bodies of victims of Nazi brutality were buried. There was no alternative but to open a grave or some graves and attempt to make an identification. Zosia contacted me to report that this activity was attracting too much attention from Germans in the area or troops passing by. I asked her to stage a funeral, with a horse-drawn hearse and pallbearers to cover their excavation of the grave. Zosia reported the ploy worked, but the news was bad. The grave contained nine bodies, one of which was Maria's. Some hair and cloth from her dress was cut and taken to Warsaw for Rossenberg's identification. I don't recall how the information came to us, but Zosia was able to learn that Maria had been arrested by the Gestapo and taken to their headquarters in Zakopane. While in a room alone waiting interrogation, she had strangled herself with a belt from her dress she tied to a doorknob.

In the aftermath of this sad episode, Rossenberg had to change apartments and, for the most part, go underground. I tried to visit him occasionally to cheer him up, but I think he seemed to have lost his will to live. He gave me an unusual pin and asked me to wear it. It was a small silver skull with two rubies for eyes. He explained that wearing it would serve as a signal to British intelligence to contact me. As luck would have it, the pin was stolen two months later while I was on a streetcar. So, I wondered, what could happen now. In the end, nothing did, of course, and my chance to become a British operative was thwarted.

Soon after these events, Rossenberg was arrested by the Gestapo in Warsaw. The circumstances were not known, but I tried every means to find out about his status. Risking everything, I contacted my only unofficial link to the Gestapo, a man who, amazingly, had approached me a few months earlier with an offer to be of service. (This story is yet to come.) In the end, this alleged Gestapo officer was able to inform me that Rossenberg had been reported by an informant to be a Jew in hiding. In fact, the letter, signed by the informant, a maid working in the apartment building, was turned over to me. "Because Jews killed Christ," she wrote, "he must be arrested and punished." So Edward Rossenberg had been betrayed, not as collaborator and friend of Poland, but as a Jew. This was a great frustration for me, and one of the saddest days of my life. I had lost a good friend and a teacher. I could not let the memory of Edward and Maria go without seeking revenge against this traitor. I set myself to the task of assassination. In the end, however, I was dissuaded by my fellow conspirators, who said that such an act would again draw the unwanted attention of the Gestapo and create trouble for us. I reluctantly agreed, so this woman was able to go on living. Perhaps, I thought, after Germany's surrender someone from the underground would remember and she might yet meet a justified fate.

Through a common association of graduates or students of the Warsaw Institute of Technology, I was involved during late 1943 and early 1944 with Group 21, Battalion 1, of the AK. They were a particularly aggressive group of officers in charge: Major Gieniak, Captain Zajac, Lieutenant Janek, Lieutenant Jerzy and my friend Officer Cadet Witold Puc. They specialized in assorted hit and run attacks and sabotage operations.

My attention during this time was diverted to some extent by organizing the "WKSB, Battalion Gdansk," or the Military Security Corps, in more formal military terms. It was a collection of a half-dozen criminals — "desperados" really — who were willing to perform violent deeds without restriction or conscience. We organized training in martial arts, knife throwing and other such subjects at two houses, on Ogrodowa 9 Street and Piusa XI 15 Street, then put them in reserve, to be activated on call for specific operations. I used two men in one operation to bomb a German Mercedes sedan transporting German officers on regular runs between various military units. The car was vulnerable as there were no escort vehicles. At a midday hour, we kept a watch for the car near an intersection on Aleje Ujazdowskie. Finally, after two hours, our patience paid off. As the car slowed for the intersection, we stepped out from behind a wall and rolled three grenades under the car. Two hit their mark, as the car lurched upward off its wheels. The three of us immediately separated in different directions. I ran into a nearby apartment building where I could watch the street from an upper floor. I knew the Germans would be sending out a patrol within minutes, so I walked out of the area as quickly as I could. The real risk in conducting these attacks was the expectation there would be revenge killings by the Gestapo. This was the price we paid because our attacks would not cease.

CHAPTER 4

The Bookstore

For a time early in my underground life, I took on the "specialty" operation of stealing maps from German facilities. Sometimes maps were passed to me via courier links in Warsaw. The maps were all sent up the chain of command for analysis. The exchanges often occurred in a bookstore I visited with increasing frequency through 1940 and 1941. Another AK operative by the name of Paszynski was the most active in "procurement," picking up those maps from behind the toilet in the bookstore, where I had placed them for him earlier. Interestingly enough, many years later he came to visit a close friend of his in Denver, Colorado, a friend, as it turned out, who was also a good friend of mine. One day both of them showed up at my home in Boulder, Colorado, and it was then, during our conversation, that it surfaced he was the very same mysterious AK operative by the name of Janusz Paszynski who had been picking up the maps I had hidden in the bookstore.

Before the war, I collected antique Russian maps from czarist times, as well as from England. I also collected books on travel, serious publications that reached 1,001 volumes in my collection. It reached the point that, in order to make room for one more book, I had to sell or otherwise remove one, so that the collection stayed at 1,001. The bookstore where I normally traded suggested I investigate another bookstore that specialized in German publications. Thus, I was led to the *Deutsche Buchhandlung Warschau* on Nowy Swiat Street. On my first visit, I found three rare books and brought them to the cashier's counter. A German officer, who appeared senior in rank, noticed one particular book I had selected and offered to buy it. I politely declined his offer and the conversation ended.

On my next visit a few days later, I noticed new book arrivals from Germany on display and a few rare editions from France. However, on

44

this visit, my attention was drawn to a door at the back of the bookstore that seemed to be attracting German officers. No other customers were going through the door. I asked one of the clerks if that room was a section for special German books. My question was met with only a shrug. My visits there apparently were frequent enough that one afternoon the owner felt comfortable enough to ask if I would watch the front counter while he ran an errand across the street. When I saw he had crossed the street, and there were no German officers in the store, I walked quickly to the back and opened the door. What I discovered there were German military manuals for operating or maintaining vehicles — tanks, aircraft and other military equipment. I recall that one was for the Messerschmitt ME-109 fighters that had marauded our skies and airbases during the invasion. I made a decision on the spot to attempt to smuggle out two or three manuals each time I visited the store. I would take the manuals, put them together in a bag with other purchases, and hope that I wouldn't be caught. My superiors in the AK seemed to be pleased with my new-found treasure trove, so I was encouraged to continue stealing selected manuals.

One afternoon, fortunately before I had entered the back room, I walked by three German officers, all colonels or lieutenant colonels. Two were army Panzerkorp officers and one Luftwaffe. One of the army officers moved in my direction and asked, if by chance, I read the *Völkischer Beobachter* newspaper. I replied that I did occasionally, when actually I read it every day as a way of keeping up with news on the war, at least as the Germans reported it. He then asked me, "Then what do you think about the war as it now stands?" At the time, German forces were pressing their attack on Stalingrad. The other panzer officer puffed up, declaring, "Whatever the circumstances, Hitler will win the war!" I decided to plunge in: "Well, I think Hitler will be destroyed and that he will lose the war!" The second panzer officer obviously felt an insult had been delivered, as he reached to unholster his sidearm. The first officer cautioned him by holding his arm down: "Let's listen and see what he has to say. I'd like to know." So, there I was, giving my first public analysis of the war — in a German establishment, and to three senior German officers.

"German ground and air forces are now stretched to the limit," I said. The invasion routes should have been through regions where there was less defensive infrastructure and less resistance from the civilian population, such as in Gruzja. Oil fields, such as in Baku, should have been seized in first strikes, and again through friendly areas, not those of enemies. Air supply by the Luftwaffe is too limited in tonnage and conditions on the ground." The friendly colonel looked down, shaking his head: "Yes you may be right, we are suffering some heavy losses." That was enough for the other panzer officer, as he patted his holster and stomped away. The other colonel asked about my family and, shaking hands, we said good-bye.

Just as the officers were leaving, I saw through the store's front window a friend leaving an apartment building across the street. I had been looking for Wanda Fejgin for weeks. She was a lovely Jewish girl, and one of the few, if not the only, female students in WIT's chemistry department. She was not involved in the underground, so far as I knew — sooner or later I would have known that — but for some reason I felt protective of her. There had been two unfortunate incidents in which she had observed, by chance, my talking to German soldiers or officers on the street, and I believe one occasion was in front of the bookstore. Both times, she immediately ran away, down a narrow side street or into a building, and disappeared from my sight. My efforts to run after her failed. The consequence of this was that she likely was left with the impression that I was collaborating with the Germans. This was extremely bothersome to me and the reason I kept up my search for her. I immediately left the bookstore, dashed across the street and entered the apartment building. The names on the mailboxes gave me no clue as to whether she lived there. For several weeks thereafter, I kept a close watch on the building, without success. Finally my frequent presence there came to the attention of my AK superiors, who ordered me to cease my surveillance. I was never able to see her again and, to this day, it distresses me greatly that we parted under such a cloud of suspicion. Coming home that afternoon, I told my mother about these incidents and asked if she could find some way to find and help Wanda. As I recall, I don't believe the opportunity ever came.

During this time, and over three years, our family was harboring a Jewish man at our Black Creek estate. My aunt Zofia, the sister of my father, handled this matter, arranging to house him with the keeper or manager of the estate, who was sworn to secrecy. Our guest worked as a farm laborer right under the eyes of the Germans occupying the manor house. Had Wanda feared for her life, as I am sure she must have, I would have not hesitated to give the same help to her, if needed.

In the meantime, I continued the theft of military manuals at the bookstore, surprisingly without incident. I would simply take one or two manuals and put them together with other purchases, and it was never noticed or questioned. Finally, I came to the conclusion that perhaps I wasn't stealing after all. It was all too casual. In fact, it was possible that the contents of the rear store room was a black market even for the German army — that is, an inventory of needed manuals that were not available in normal German supply channels. Speculating further, I wondered if perhaps the store owner was anti–Hitler and he was with us.

Then one day came when I noticed a new arrival, a beautiful large book of black and white photos of the picturesque Dolomite and Alps mountains. The gold-colored cover was inscribed with the title *Das Goldene Buch der Berge*. I simply knew I had to have it. I told the store owner, "I would like to buy the book today, whatever your price." He replied, "That's impossible, it was ordered especially by Governor Frank." He was referring to Governor-General Hans Frank, the head of the General Government of Poland — that part of Poland to the west not formally annexed by Germany in the aftermath of the invasion.

I decided to challenge him: "All right, let me use your phone, I'm going to call a general in the Gestapo." I called the officer, whose name, Nicolaus, had been given to me by Ilsa Glinicka, the wife of senior German civilian official attached to the General Government, as a point of contact at their headquarters on Aleja Szucha. "Sir, this is Rosinski, and I am calling at Ilsa's suggestion. I am in a German bookstore and I have the most

Das Goldene Buch der Berge (The Golden Book of Mountains)

beautiful book, simply fantastic." And I described it to him. "If you instruct the owner to sell it to me, I'll bring it to you, so you can give it to her as a gift."

Without hesitating, Nicolaus replied, "Give the phone to the owner." Then all I heard from the owner was, "Ya wohl, Herr General, ya wohl!" The brief conversation ended with a sharp clicking of heels, all in good form. The owner turned to me with a slight grimace as he said, "Here, you take it without payment — compliments of the store." I took the book to Gestapo headquarters and left it with an officer for Nicolaus. I did not see him at that visit, and in fact, I'd never seen him in person. Thus therein lies the still unsolved mystery of his fate — and not only of Nicolaus, but of Ilsa as well.

Ilsa called me later to thank me for the book. "But," she said, "the most important thing is that Governor Frank will never have it. We have intercepted it." A few days later Ilsa gave me this book as a gift. For a young German woman, perhaps three or four years older than I, that proved to be an interesting revelation. I admired this spirited and attractive woman but at the same time feared where her life had taken her. I knew that she lived in Poland before the war, so she wasn't a post-invasion "import." She may also have been acquainted with my uncle Jan, but this never arose in conversation with either Jan or Ilsa. Some things I just was hesitant to ask.

My concern about and for her stemmed from sightings of Ilsa with a senior Gestapo officer in Warsaw. Presumably, the officer was Nicolaus. This eventually drew the attention of AK surveillances and AK concluded she was working for the Germans. When I learned of this, I did everything I could to dissuade them from targeting her for assassination. I even moved temporarily to her apartment so that I could better protect her from AK hotheads. What I could not tell them, for fear of a leak, was my conclusion she worked for British intelligence. My first thought early on was that she must be Nicolaus' lover. However, as our private conversations continued that seemed highly unlikely. Ilsa knew I kept unusual hours, acted rather independently as a displaced university student, and possessed "official" German credentials, easily obtained from her husband. She also had access to an official car, which gave her protected mobility throughout the city. One day, when she visited my apartment, our discussion finally prompted her to smile and blurt out, "OK, you must be working with us!" Since she obviously was not working for the Germans, and she wasn't an AK operative, her unspoken loyalty rested with the British. Without responding, I moved to her side and kissed her. So, this is how we sealed a "pact of nonaggression." We did settle the matter of General Nicolaus, who for me remained a "telephone voice." Ilsa told me emphatically, "Jan, don't ever ask me to sleep with Nicolaus." Of course, that was far from my mind.

These are the last recollections I have of Ilsa. I received a telephone call from my mother in Warsaw in 1953 when I was living in Chicago, informing me that Ilsa had passed away. She provided no details and I have no idea how she came by this information. Ilsa would have been only in her mid–30s, with much of her life to come. I do recall that in Warsaw in 1943 my mother cautioned me more than once about maintaining a relationship, even friendship, with Ilsa. Her concern was based largely on Ilsa's being German and uncertainties about where her loyalties resided. For me, it was not a matter of doubt about my security, but Ilsa's.

A few years later, in Boulder, Colorado, a member of my family in Warsaw sent me *Das Goldene Buch der Berge* without explanation as to how it was obtained. It remains a constant reminder of Ilsa and the question as to what might have happened to this brave young woman.

CHAPTER 5

The Governor-General

Returning safely to Berlin from his one-day visit to Warsaw on October 5, 1939, to view his victorious army, Hitler must have renewed his venomous determination to reduce the Polish people to slavery. We Poles knew we could expect harsh treatment in the months to come; that it might be years we could not yet contemplate. We had no knowledge of the depth of his hatred as he infused the Nazi faithful with his extremism, and especially the security forces — the Gestapo, SS (*Schutzstaffel*), or Security Staff, and SA (*Sturmabteilung*), storm troops or Assault Force.

The carving up of Poland into three territories would be hidden in the secret annex of the German-Soviet Non-Aggression Treaty, signed in Moscow by von Ribbentrop and Molotov on August 23, 1939. The more official name of the pact was the German-Soviet Boundary and Friendship Treaty. In reality, it had more to do with the redefined Polish borders than those of the two signatories. The Western Territory, with its four provinces, was named Warthegau; the Central or Middle territory became the General Government of Poland; and the Eastern territory, including Wilno (Lithuania presently), and Lwow (Ukraine now), came under the control of the Red Army. But more important for the Fuehrer's territorial ambitions, the treaty paved the way for Germany to launch Operation White against Poland on September 1, and the attack across Poland's eastern frontier by the Soviets on September 17, 1939. Again, by the terms of the treaty, Poland would cease to exist, at least in the minds of the two conquerors.

One of Hitler's first administrative acts was to appoint longtime party hack Hans Frank, who headed the Nazi Party's Legal Affairs Office, as Governor-General of Poland. Frank was a typical example of the Nazi intellectual gangster. He had joined the party in 1927, soon after his graduation from law school, and quickly made a reputation as the legal light of the movement. Nimble-minded, energetic, well read not only in the law but in general literature, devoted to the arts and especially to music, he became a power in the legal profession after the Nazis assumed office, serving first as Bavarian Minister of Justice, then "Reichsminister without Portfolio" and president of the Academy of Law and the German Bar Association. A dark, dapper, bouncy fellow, father of five children, his intelligence and cultivation partly offset his primitive fanaticism and up to that time made him one of the least repulsive men around Hitler. But behind the civilized veneer of the man lay the cold killer. The forty-two volume journal he kept of his life and works, which showed up at the Nuremberg Trials, was one of the most terrifying documents to come out of the dark Nazi world, portraying the author as an icy, efficient, ruthless, bloodthirsty man. "The Poles," he declared one day after he took his new job, "shall be the slaves of the German Reich." While the Gestapo and SS were tasked with liquidating the Jews, Frank's job, besides squeezing food and supplies and forced labor out of Poland, was to liquidate the intelligentsia. As justification for this task, he quoted Hitler's directive: "The men capable of leadership in Poland must be liquidated. Those following them ... must be eliminated in their turn. There is no need to burden the Reich with this ... no need to send these elements to Reich concentration camps" (William L. Shirer, *The Rise and Fall of the Third Reich*, pp. 661–662).

The General Government of Poland was established by Hitler's decree on October 12, 1939, and Hans Frank assumed his post as governor-general under the same decree. His temporary headquarters would be the eighteenth century baroque-style Belvedere Palace in Warsaw, the traditional residence of Polish kings and rulers two miles from the city center. Belvedere was in a beautiful park setting, with the added attraction of public baths and tennis courts, where I played before the war. With the occupation, I concluded it was no longer appropriate to enjoy such leisure. Frank would soon relocate to the Royal Palace in Krakow, where the occupation intended to create a new capital. In any event, Frank's presence at Belvedere gave me one more opportunity to conduct a spy mission.

My AK superiors ordered me to conduct a surveillance of the palace, officials and cars coming and going and any unusual activity that might warrant the AK's immediate attention. I decided to recruit Nata and use the same pumpkin or sunflower seed ploy we had used for surveillance of the restaurant in Warsaw that was frequented by German army personnel. The risks, however, were higher, given the armed guard contingent around the palace and patrols along the streets leading to it. Nonetheless, we managed to observe the scene for three or four days before terminating the activity. However, during this time, I had worked myself into a mental state that demanded bold action. Without rational deliberation, I marched off to the palace on my way to demand an audience with the governor-general. Somehow, I managed to pass through the outer cordon of guards and the security officers in the palace itself. I was wearing my ever-present school hat and long heavy coat, which might have lent me an official appearance. In any event, I made it past Frank's aide and found myself in the governor-general's office.

Only because Frank was likely speechless, I had my say, short as it was, about the hardships already meted out harshly by the German army and the need to improve food rationing. I thought I would be thrown out or jailed, but I was escorted to the front gate, released and told not to attempt this foolish act again. Nata was most upset with my risk taking, but not nearly as much as my mother when I told her of the incident that evening at home. We all knew, without specific knowledge of orders or directives from Berlin, that Poland's educated and professional class had been marked for elimination. Similar acts or actions directed toward the university and secondary school students were also suspected. The edict closing all such educational facilities was proof enough, but mass actions against students per se were harder to discern. The roundups of Polish youth, especially those with "Aryan traits," and their movement to Germany was yet to come.

General Hans Frank had far from a free hand in administering the occupation government in Poland, first briefly from Warsaw and then from Krakow. His deputy, Arthur Seyss-Inquart, who had served previously as Governor of Austria, was not heard from publicly; he was also a lawyer and yet another toady to Hitler and the Nazi party. After Frank moved his office to Krakow in late October 1939, Warsaw was governed by Ludwig Fischer, a lawyer as well, who held the rank of SA-Gruppenführer (lieutenant general). There were other Gestapo and SS officers who soon enough made their presence known in the capital through misdeeds against the populace. SS-Brigadeführer (major general) Franz Kutschera and SS-Brigadeführer Jürgen Stroop were two such officers, and they will make their appearance later in my story.

Early in his administration, Frank came under intense pressure from Berlin to make shipments of agricultural goods to Germany, as well as making agricultural products available for consumption by German occupation troops. This entailed forcing Polish farmers off their land and the recruitment of forced farm labor. In his first month as governor-general, Frank informed the army of Hitler's orders:

Poland can only be administered by utilizing the country through means of ruthless exploitation, deportation, of all supplies, raw materials, machines, factory installations, etc., which are important for the German war economy, availability of all workers for work within Germany, reduction of the entire Polish economy to absolute minimum necessary for bare existence of the population, closing of all educational institutions, especially technical schools, and colleges in order to prevent growth of the new Polish intelligentsia. Poland shall be treated as a colony. "The Poles shall be the slaves of the Greater German World Empire" [Shirer, p. 944].

Most, if not all, Polish landowners and land-owning farmers in Germany's annexed territory were expelled to the General Government. In many instances, they, in turn, took over lands from Jewish owners, who were subjected to mass relocation to concentrated living areas, such as the ghetto in Warsaw. Deputy Governor Ludwig Fischer was known to have taken a lead in organizing these movements. Food rationing set a near starvation diet for most Poles but caused the situation to become even more onerous for the Jews in the ghetto, who would be cut off from food sources. Another population group to be denied sustenance was a more convenient decision for the Third Reich — Russian prisoners of war.

In the spring of 1940, the occupation regime imposed a food rationing policy whereby Germans would be allowed 2,600 calories daily, Poles 670 and Jews 184. This translated into rapid malnutrition and death by starvation for those of us under the boot. Yet, the ingenuity and determination of our people found ways to provide enough food to survive. Taking some risk and banking on enough fluency in German, I occasionally waited in lines at German rationing stores, using stolen ration coupons. More often, however, I would trek to outlying villages by taking the narrow-gauge train, which was surprisingly free of police controls. I was fairly well known in two villages not far from our Black Creek estate and usually found a supply of potatoes, vegetables and a piece of meat or kielbasa. I would pack the food carefully in my rucksack and a small suitcase and hope for the best. When I boarded the train, I would place them in the overhead rack, but a seat or two away so as to look like they did not belong to me. Bread, however, was the mainstay of our diet. Bread was also potentially dangerous, especially in carrying fresh baked loaves under cover. German soldiers were well seasoned to the smell of fresh bread, and if provoked, they would not hesitate to follow an inviting aroma to its source. Fortunately, my mother and I evaded detection. She would also bake bread at home and hide the loaves inside a coal stove in the apartment.

Three years into the occupation we began to exhaust some food supplies, even though Poland functioned on an agricultural economy. The year 1943 served up a bitterly cold winter and food availability reflected it. Sometimes we were reduced to one meal a day, perhaps some horse meat and soup. Then later we turned to spoiled or dried vegetables, and eventually dogs and even cats. I recall that one of my AK comrades attracted a friendly dog that was quickly reduced to stew meat and was surprisingly tasty. Soon enough we found out that the dog was a pet of one of our senior commanders. He was completely upset, but it was obviously too late to do anything about it. As I was not particularly fond of dogs, I did not assume any sense of guilt. Little did I know at the time that my life would be saved by a friendly German police dog, but that is a story yet to come. Roasted pigeon was a particular delicacy in our diets. I had an air gun I used occasionally to shoot pigeons on the street or in a field. This proved to be a popular sport of necessity, so it wasn't long before pigeons disappeared from Warsaw and outlying areas.

Unknown to us at the time were the even more punitive starvation measures that would soon be imposed in the occupied Ukraine as the Wehrmacht's Operation Barbarossa rolled across the Soviet Union. As a link in our courier system, I received and passed on to my AK superiors a highly secret German document outlining a strategy to re-create the Ukraine as a bread basket for the Third Reich. Once under total control of the German army, the rich agricultural lands would be claimed without compensation and reallocated as private estates to German military commanders as a reward for their loyal service to the Fuehrer. Ukrainian farmers would be retained in the short term to train the new German landowners and then killed off without trace. The scale of such barbarity was hard to contemplate. We discussed it at our underground meetings, but there was nothing we could do but continue our own fight as best we could.

On top of seizures of Polish lands, the occupation imposed a taxation system that left nothing untouched. Taxes on marginal wages were even levied on Polish slave laborers in Germany. Within a few months, the growing opposition to these oppressive taxes finally reached the governor-general's office. Eventually, the German administrators in Warsaw, as well as the leadership in Berlin, chose to ease up on levying some of the taxes for fear that they would stiffen the Polish resistance movement.

Yet Frank was likely caught in a position where, surrounded by virtually independent hierarchies of Gestapo and SS commands, he was under pressure to exact punishing results from occupied Poland. Basically insecure, and with his authority threatened by a constant power struggle with the SS, Frank compensated for his weakness with exaggerated brutality.

He supervised the slaughter of the Polish intelligentsia, shipped hundreds of thousands of slave laborers to the Reich, and provided the sites for several of the most notorious death camps, including Auschwitz, Treblinka, and Sobibor, proclaiming that his mission was to rid Poland of lice and Jews (Anthony Read, *The Devil's Disciples*, p. 3).

Little did we know that my family would be caught up in Hitler's grand scheme of destruction. Shortly before transferring his office to Krakow, Hans Frank summoned my uncle Jan Rosinski to a private meeting at Belvedere Palace. Jan had no idea why the governor-general had called for the meeting, but there were no good reasons to consider. I suspected Jan was active in the underground. The family was alerted to the summons, and we all held our breaths. A few hours later, Jan called me to meet him at his apartment to discuss the events of that morning. He was still nearly in a state of shock, and after hearing the story of the meeting, so was I. On arrival, he was immediately escorted into Hans Frank's office. The governor-general got right down to business. He called on Jan straightaway to form and to guide a new government for the territory of the General Government. Jan said he was astounded and completely speechless. Finally mustering his thoughts, he asked Frank, "How did you select me for such a position?" Trying to set him at ease, Frank responded, "When we researched your background, we discovered your ancestors were given a German coat of arms in the 17th Century. So, you have a German heritage in your family." This was not news to Jan, but he admitted he had little time to extricate himself from this very awkward situation. Jan said that, after collecting his wits, he informed Frank that he could not accept such an appointment, that he was unqualified to take such a responsibility.

This is not what the governor-general wanted to hear. "Do you realize we could have you executed for refusing to accept this appointment?" "Yes, you could easily execute me, but I don't think you will do it. There are other ways I can be useful," Jan told him. This led to another matter that was foremost on Frank's mind, and that was requisitioning agricultural lands for the exclusive production of crops for the German occupational forces. Frank admitted he was under some pressure from Berlin to provide in-country food sources — the key to their "living-off-the-land" strategy. To meet these demands, he instructed Jan to immediately submit a plan to him on what was none other than a forced takeover of private agriculture holdings in Poland.

Somehow, there had to be a way to lessen the hardship that would befall Polish farmers. Jan told me he would need to use maps in any plan, but they would have to be maps that would support restricted or limited land seizures. In order to do this, we had to gain access to the government's central records office where official maps were kept, including those in a special agricultural section. Somehow, Jan had determined that there was one key map that showed croplands. The only possible way to reduce the number or acreage to be seized would be to falsify or alter the lands identified on this particular map. Then the proposal Jan would submit to Frank would reflect a reduced estimate of suitable croplands. I told Jan to leave it me, and I would see what we could do to help.

I immediately turned to Nata, my erstwhile colleague in crime, and recruited her for this new and our heretofore most complex operation. We were able through some preliminary scouting to identify the map room and location of the map in the bound volume. Not only that, we also found a small supply of original paper the maps were made from and from which we could prepare a completely new and altered map page. Our plan was to gain admittance to the building, which was lightly guarded by two German soldiers at the entrance, and get Nata into the map room. While I and two other friends I recruited distracted the guards, Nata would then carefully cut out the map page we needed and hide it in her dress, along with some of the original paper for making an altered replacement map.

Everything went as planned. The guards suspected nothing, as I told them about my family's concerns about defining the property lines of our estate. I told them we needed to come back for one more visit in order to alleviate any suspicions. Fortune stayed with us, as I was able to find the original inks used in making the maps; so between my forgery skills and Nata's artistry we produced an acceptable falsified map. The next step in the operation was more intricate. There were also some added risks, as we needed to give time for Nata to gain access to the map room, insert the replacement map into the volume, and then exit the building without getting arrested. We finally agreed that we would revisit the facility late in the afternoon and have Nata stay in the building overnight so that she would have enough time to glue and dry the map page to be inserted. I told her she could not light a match or smoke a cigarette, make any noise or even flush a toilet: "Just stay like a mouse." We would then come back the next day and retrieve her — that is, if everything went according to plan. There did not appear to be any soldiers living in the building, there being only the guards at the front entrance and some parked army vehicles and troops on the street in front of the building. We then left the building, and I was able to sign Nata out on the visitors log without anyone noticing.

The next morning, my two friends and I returned and were able to gain entrance to the map room. Nata had slept fitfully in a storeroom during the night, only to be wakened occasionally by sounds of a toilet being used by soldiers on the main floor. She had been able to finish drying the glued page earlier that morning, so we were ready to extract her from the crime scene. We did this without incident and Nata was home free. Had she been caught, it would have been death for us all. Her unquestioned loyalty and bravery was remarkable. She was also, like myself, a fatalist when it came to the everyday challenges we faced, but a fatalist in the sense of confidence in herself to overcome any obstacles. We had to think like this to maintain our sanity, and, together with prayer, it kept us going.

For some reason, I decided not to tell my uncle that our forgery mission was successful, so he took the map volume with him without first examining it when he met again with Governor Frank. Jan had asked a close family friend, Colonel Korolkiewicz, to accompany him to the meeting. The colonel was a wealthy landowner and well versed on the subject of agricultural land use in Poland. My uncle made his presentation, and in using the redrawn map, advised the governor that there would be considerably less prime agricultural land available than they originally estimated. When he showed the map to Frank, it was the first time Jan had seen it himself. He was completely dismayed but, of course, he didn't say a thing. Apparently, Jan was able to make his report and exit the meeting without committing himself to Frank's political plans. We did meet after his meeting at Belvedere Palace. Jan expressed both his appreciation for the technical support he had received and asked how we were able to make such an authentic replacement map. We told him the map had been aged a few decades by putting it in an oven for a few minutes.

Fortunately, as far as I knew, my uncle avoided any recriminations from the "presidential" episode, as well as the land issue. I learned that Hans Frank called Jan for consultations on other occasions, but on different issues. Jan performed the minimum courtesies, but nothing more. We thought that any further meetings might offer the opportunity to assassinate Frank, but the occasion never arose. Consideration of such an act brought to mind the assassination of a German gauleiter, or mayor, in his office, which brought a reprisal killing of 5,000 Poles. This we did not want to bring down on the citizens of Warsaw.

During those early years of the occupation, there was little hope to keep us motivated, other than the well-deserved hatred of the German oppressors. Certainly, we could not have seen ahead to October 16, 1946, when it was announced that Hans Frank was one of ten Nazi officials who had been executed for their crimes. I was in London at the time finishing my degree in chemistry at Polish University College, Imperial College, when the welcome news came. Although it wasn't known at the time, it would have been impossible to visit the grave sites of General Alfred Jodl, ex–chief of operations of the Armed Forces High Command; Joachim von Ribbentrop, ex–foreign minister; Frank and seven others since their collective ashes were reportedly dumped in a roadside ditch outside Munich. Even the stark circumstances of Frank's execution could not pay for the atrocities he inflicted on the people of Poland.

CHAPTER 6

Gestapo

The origins and development of Germany's secret state police, or Gestapo, was of little concern to those of us in the underground. The simple fact was that by the time it was introduced in Poland in the fall of 1939 it had become the instrument of total oppression by the Third Reich. That it became suborned, through various political twists and turns, to the SS mattered little either. Both were deadly enemies on the streets of Warsaw. The AK offered no training or preparation in dealing with, or avoiding, the security apparatus of the occupation, so it was up to the individual and his survival instincts to remain a step ahead of the enemy. Certainly, information was shared up and down the underground command as needed, especially if it concerned critical security threats, as well as orders to counter or eliminate German operations against the resistance.

Each day, before leaving the relative safety of our apartment, I would carefully observe the scene on Marszalkowska Street from the fourth floor balcony, which afforded a strategic view in either direction. Uniformed German soldiers were easy to spot, but not so for Gestapo or SS officers in civilian clothes. Yet a keen eye could ignite a warning signal in my mind, enough at least to take countermeasures. On several occasions, after spotting soldiers or a patrol coming to my front or back, I would simply enter the nearest gate to an apartment building and dash up the stairs to the third or fourth floor. Most buildings in Warsaw had no more than five floors. If soldiers or the Gestapo entered the building and started a search, I would then select an apartment at random and ring the bell. All too frequently the person who answered the bell knew instinctively when she saw me that I needed help. My trusty school cap also helped identify me. If I met a questioning face, I would simply ask to hide there for a few minutes until the soldiers moved on. I was never refused or questioned. A few times, I was even offered tea, which I was pleased to accept — once the danger had passed. A favorite hiding place would be a large stand-up wardrobe cabinet. On one occasion, an elderly woman accepted my plea for help and helped me fold myself into a cabinet. When the officers worked their way down the hallway to her apartment and attempted to push their way in, she threw a very credible tantrum that effectively turned them away. Scowling, she opened the cabinet door, exclaiming, "I've had enough for today, now you get out of here!" I was happy to do so and live another day.

In planning my escapes, I avoided places of work or office buildings, where there was no privacy. However, going to work one morning, I had no choice but to take what you might call "passing refuge" in a diplomatic mission. I was late in spotting an oncoming troop transport loaded with armed soldiers. Some of them started firing their rifles at civilian pedestrians, including me. A bullet fragment ricocheted off a cement wall behind me, nicking my upper arm. The Swiss consulate was only a short distance away. Fortunately, the door was not guarded or locked. I dashed in, ran through the lobby past the astonished staff, and out a back door that led to a small yard bordered by a fairly high stone wall. I had trained for such challenges with leg-weight exercises, so it was not the first wall I had vaulted nor would it be the last. I made my way through a garden and bushes to the next building. I quickly climbed the stairs to the fourth floor where I had a window view of the street below. Traffic had been stopped by a German patrol. Passengers were being forced off a bus — possibly being detained or rounded up to fulfill slave labor requirements of the Third Reich.

I was horrified to see that among those passengers was an AK member and friend, Maria Piotrowska. At her request, I had given her a cyanide pill for a life-threatening emergency situation. This was the last I was to see of her, and her brother confirmed later that she had committed suicide rather than face interrogation by the Gestapo. The AK command took no official position on the use of cyanide, so it became an individual decision, if one could get access to it. Since I had access to cyanide in the institute's lab, the AK requested that I supply a small amount to them, no questions asked. I asked my friend Natalia ("Nata") Leszczynska to go to the lab and bring me what she could find. The next day she showed up at my apartment with a large package that weighed nearly 20 pounds, all cyanide. I was astounded, but I did not ask her where she found such a large amount. Before passing it on to the AK, I extracted a small amount and put it in a glass vial for safekeeping back at the lab. It was from this vial that I gave a pill to Maria. When she asked me for it, I was very hostile to the idea and told her pointedly, "You should not be thinking of killing yourself, but only fighting this enemy to the end!" Her response was to tell me to mind my own business and simply do what she had asked. To this day I am haunted by this tragedy, as I feel some responsibility for her death.

With the late winter chill of 1940 still in the air, I came upon a street beggar sitting by the front gate to our apartment building. He looked to be an unusual beggar, however, as he was wearing the same school cap I wore. I asked him directly, "How is it you have to beg, if you attended such a prestigious school as the Warsaw Institute of Technology?" I got no answer in reply, but a look from a murderous face, a real thug. For certain, he was not, nor had ever been, a WIT student. To be sure, I called Nata and two or three other classmates and asked them to stop by my apartment building and take a look at this fellow to see if they recognized him as a fellow student. He failed the test. The next morning when I left the apartment, he had moved his beggar act to the next street; but then he got in a Gestapo car, never to be seen again. It turned out he had been watching an apartment building across the street. When I realized this, I immediately entered the building lobby to check the names on each mailbox. I was surprised to see the family name of a classmate of mine, Dziankowski, and an expert organic chemist I knew of by the name of Dr. Boehm.

I knocked on Witold Dziankowski's door and alerted him to the danger of the surveillance. I strongly suggested that the beggar fellow had to be eliminated; either he should do it, or I would have to do the job. The next day, I noticed a large spot of blood that had been washed away from where the "beggar" had perched on the street. Nothing was ever said, but I should have been alerted to the fact that my classmate was also in the underground. A day later, he mentioned to me about an operation he was conducting, assuming correctly that I also was in the AK. After double checking for any surveillance, he took me to a small chemical factory, but it had a large laboratory. He and some cohorts had stolen a railway car loaded with ether that they planned to convert to ethyl alcohol to sell for batteries, to sell to hospitals, and to use as an explosive to destroy German military vehicles and tanks. They had built a secret opening to the lab, which was equipped with some devices and supplies collected from WIT's chemical department and laboratory. I told my uncle Jan I would be occupied for some time working in a lab, not further identified to him.

However, this effort would come to an early end after the factory came under surveillance by the Gestapo. Fortunately for me, this occurred just before I started working there. My classmate Witold and his brother were arrested and sent to a concentration camp. Nothing more was heard from them, and Witold's father informed me weeks later that they had been executed. Also, Dr. Boehm simply disappeared, and I accepted that as positive news that he had escaped through the underground. Although I escaped my own fate by perhaps no more than a day, my thoughts and prayers remained centered on these three brave men.

Soon after this setback, a Jewish man who lived in our apartment building, actually on the same floor, committed suicide. I thought defensively, in that there may have been serious concerns behind the death. However, my suspicions were alleviated when the maintenance man for the building told me that the man had been arrested and interrogated and could not face the prospect of another arrest and torture. Sadly, suicide was his answer. Our apartment building yielded up yet another incident, and this one even more bizarre. Later, one evening in the early spring of 1941, I was climbing the stairs to our fourth floor apartment, looking forward to a quiet dinner with my mother. As I reached the third floor landing, a well-presented man looked to be waiting for me. He was a Pole, or spoke as one with a higher education, and appeared to be in his early forties. He introduced himself and showed me his Gestapo ID papers. Visions of a quiet dinner immediately vaporized.

Before I could come out of shock, he smiled and said, "Sir, here are my credentials, I am from the Gestapo. I would like to offer my help, if needed. I cannot get you or anyone out of a concentration camp, but if you have some other serious problem, I will do anything under the sun to help." Needless to say, I remained near speechless. As I recall, he didn't press the matter further, and I needed to create some distance between us. Suddenly, however, I concluded that this likely was not a provocation. He had an apartment on the third floor, which I started watching in my comings and goings. It did not appear to be fully furnished, so perhaps it was a temporary residence, or a place where he kept a woman. However, we never saw a woman or anyone else visiting his apartment. It would take some time before I trusted him enough to ask for his help in an emergency. First, I had to answer the question of "why me?" I could only conclude that he recognized my family name on the mailbox and acquired enough background information on the Rosinski's for his satisfaction. I regret that today I do not recall his name. I decided at the time not to report the incident to my AK command, which may not have been the wisest decision ever, but obviously I remained alive.

It seemed that every day brought a new challenge or a new mystery, either to solve or avoid. Not far from our apartment, I spotted a rather attractive Polish woman wearing silk hosiery. She was standing at a bus stop at an early morning hour, which gave me the opportunity to observe her. Nearly a year into the occupation, no woman could wear such luxury unless it came from German largess. I asked Nata to follow her from the bus stop the next day, or until we could acquire some information about her. From that first day, Nata concluded the woman was worthy of our attention — she was also wearing an expensive French perfume. "OK," I said, "but let's go slowly at first and see what she's all about." I asked Witold Puc, another classmate and AK member, to try to make social contact with her. Witold was not a "ladies' man," so I didn't hold high prospects for results from this ploy. Finally, we were able to determine the woman was German, so out of reach for us. Nevertheless, such happenings reflected our heightened sense of security — for ourselves, as well as the underground.

While I was devoting some time to my cover job on Smolna Street as a food supplier to the occupation, I received a telephone call from the father of a WIT classmate, Wlodek Krynicki. In a trembling voice, he alerted me that Gestapo officers had just come and arrested Wlodek. He and I had participated in one of our first operations, which was spiking the bearings in the wheels of railway cars with carborundum. This abrasive substance had the effect of grinding the surface of bearings, and thus eventually seizing up the wheels. This was a high risk operation which involved the cover ploy of walking a dog in a rail yard and getting close enough to the train wheels to use an injector device to get the carborundum into the bearing assemblies. Wlodek's sister was also involved in the operation. We preferred to conduct the operation at night, but then we couldn't see the train wheels clearly to see what we were doing. The irregular presence of Wehrmacht security guards in the rail yards were our most serious concerns. Despite these risks, we could measure our success by the several railcars that were pushed into the maintenance shops for repairs, all making noticeable noises of friction.

The first question the Gestapo asked Wlodek was, "Who is this Rosinski fellow?" The father said that Wlodek explained I was a classmate at WIT, a friend, and that I worked part time as a food supplier to the German military, and was also involved in growing some seed crops, such as wheat and rye, as well as potatoes. He warned me not to return home until the matter could be investigated. I thanked him, and then telephoned Ilsa, my contact with the ever illusive Gestapo officer General Nicolaus. "Look here," I told her, "the problem is this: a friend was arrested today by the Gestapo and they asked about me. Perhaps I should go home, because if

I don't, it might cast some suspicion on me. Sooner or later they could arrest me. So, I'll go home and if everything is all right, I'll call you. If not, and I walk into a trap, I'll call my uncle Jan and he can call you for help." With worry in her voice, Ilsa replied, "Jan, I'll do anything to help you, but don't ask me to sleep with that man!" So I reassured her that would not be asked of her or expected.

Later that afternoon, as I approached my apartment building, I saw Gestapo cars parked on the street. (These were usually black Mercedes sedans.) As I passed through the lobby entrance and up the stairway to the second floor, there was a Gestapo officer standing there, smoking a cigarette. To check his identity, I asked him in German for the time of day, and he replied in German that it was a few minutes after six. He did not question me, so I continued to the third floor, encountering another officer, and the same on the fourth floor. When my mother let me in, I could see she was in tears and a nervous wreck.

"The Gestapo is everywhere, on the street and in the building, they're all over," she told me. "Do you have a gun with you or in the apartment?"

"No, I don't," I replied, "so don't worry. I have done nothing and belong to nothing, so nothing can happen to me!"

Still showing signs of extreme stress, she lashed out. "If I'd known you were such a coward, I would have killed you when you were born!"

I tried to make light of such an outburst. "Well, as long as I'm still alive, why don't we go ahead and have dinner?"

"I don't understand why at a time like this, you can even think of eating!"

"Look, I'm very hungry, and it's time to eat."

Before she could reply, there suddenly was a big commotion outside in the center courtyard. I looked through the curtains of the front window and saw Gestapo officers arresting a young woman who had an apartment across the courtyard from us. I had kept an eye on her over several weeks, not only because she was pretty and probably only in her early 20s, but because I suspected she was more than just a student or some office worker. In the days that followed her arrest, I made some discreet inquiries and learned that she had been a courier for the AK between Warsaw and Krakow. She was never seen again. I also learned from Wlodek Krynicki's father that Wlodek had been executed in the concentration camp. Another dedicated and loyal student in the AK lost to our German overlords. For some unknown reason, the Gestapo never pursued me further than questioning Wlodek about me. Perhaps, their interest in me was aroused by our apartment being in the same building as the woman who was arrested.

I was just grateful to live another day. I did approach the mysterious Gestapo officer who had offered his services about Wlodek's arrest, but there was nothing he could do.

So, these became the conditions under which we lived from day to day in Warsaw. Even within a closed family, we could not divulge to each other our respective secret commitments to the underground. While such rigid discipline sometimes strained personal relationships, it had the larger effect of protecting the AK from penetration by the enemy. Again, it is the dictum and safety net for all: "What you don't know, won't hurt you — or others."

Also, early in the occupation, we faced other risks not necessarily directed against the Germans. One such activity was to organize an underground medical school, allowing as many medical school students at Warsaw University as possible to continue their education and thus serve the Polish people and the AK with badly needed medical care. The university had been shut down since the first days of the occupation, but we were able to get access to one building with a laboratory where we could conduct classes. Dr. Zaorski, a senior staff member of the medical school, led this effort; thus it became known informally as the Zaorski School of Medicine. I accepted an appointment as a lecturer in chemistry, learning from Barbara Natorff-Tokarczyk, a student and my wife-to-be, that I was most despised by all the students for my difficult examinations and strict grading. Actually, that made me feel that I must have been a success.

It would have been unrealistic for us to believe that such an enterprise could continue undetected by the Gestapo. This was brought to our attention, and shock, one evening at the school when Gestapo agents rushed into a classroom of students and shot the lecturer, leaving him to die at the lectern. As the gun smoke cleared the air, the agents immediately left without a word and without arresting anyone. The class was left to contact the family and dispose of the body. What to make of yet another bizarre and tragic incident? The lecturer, as it turned out, was Jewish, but we could not be certain this factored in the assassination. What became both puzzling and clear at the same time was that no moves were made by German security to close the school, so they must have determined that there was some residual advantage in having more qualified doctors, even Polish ones, available for medical services that the Germans could not provide, even in some cases for themselves. In any event, Barbara, who was in the classroom where the murder took place, later became a skilled surgeon, after graduating from the Warsaw University "Underground School of Medicine."

The Gestapo showed its skills in penetrating Polish society in other ways. Modern-day espionage might refer to this as creating a false front to entrap AK operatives to work for an alleged AK-allied organization. This was the Sword and the Plow, in Polish *Miecz i Plug*. There is more than one story as to the origins or formation of this organization, but it is likely that it was the brainchild of a Gestapo officer. Instances of collaboration with German authorities were rare, if they occurred at all. However, two elements within the Sword and Plow conspired to promote Polish-German underground cooperation to fight the Red Army and also the Polish resistance. This effort was cut short by the execution of three Polish conspirators in September 1943 (Norman Davies, *Rising '44*, p. 111).

What made the Sword and Plow personal for me was that my friend Jerzy Robak became actively involved as a leader, either recruited or voluntarily. As it would turn out, I would overlook much in our friendship to see that he was spared from AK countermeasures. Interestingly enough, it was another friend and classmate who confirmed my first suspicions that the Sword and Plow was a bastard child of the Gestapo. My friend Wlodek Dahlig had become infatuated with a beautiful woman he thought to be Polish and above all suspicion. Without yet confiding in him, I had learned that she was not Polish but Ukrainian, despite her language skills. I also had collected some information on her probable collaboration with the Gestapo. When I confronted Wlodek with this information, he exploded in anger. Calming him down, I said, "Look, you might be right, but I also may be right. So, for your safety let's investigate her apartment, and see what we can find." Wlodek thought for a moment, then agreed. We both knew she was away on a trip to Vienna. However, Wlodek thought her travel was personal, while I had information that she was at Gestapo headquarters in Vienna. Her clandestine travel there would soon have even more sinister meaning.

I told Wlodek that there wasn't a locked door in Warsaw that I couldn't go through, so we were able to enter the woman's apartment without being heard or noticed. We started off with a quick search and came up with nothing. I could see that Wlodek felt relieved, but I caught him up short: "We've obviously missed something, so let's start again." He objected, but then finally agreed to help me. We searched particularly closely in all the cabinets, but still found nothing. I told Wlodek that we were doing something wrong, so we must try again. This time, he was really upset and sat down. I went into the woman's wardrobe and searched through her dresses. In the lower part of the wardrobe, I spotted a small cabinet. After searching all the drawers, I discovered one that had a hollow sound on the bottom. It turned out to be a false bottom which contained official German documents. One was the woman's papers identifying her as a Gestapo officer — officer, not agent!

Wlodek nearly fainted. He couldn't imagine he had been completely duped by this obviously "talented" woman. Finally, in a daze, he admitted, "Well, now I have to believe you." Trying to ease his shock, I replied, "That's life. I will do everything I can to protect her, and that will be in our interests, as she mustn't suspect anything. So, first we must restore everything we touched to where it was originally." Since this would take some time, I told Wlodek we should not risk leaving the apartment in daylight or after curfew, so we must stay overnight and leave in the morning. Wlodek, at my urging, did continue the relationship with the officer, but, as anyone could imagine, his heart was not in it.

This diversion of espionage did not bring an end to my suspicions of the Sword and Plow; it was only the beginning. It was in the late winter of 1943 when my friend, and also classmate, Jerzy Robak called me and asked to meet me at my apartment. He didn't explain why because that would have tipped off the Gestapo should my telephone be tapped. He arrived within minutes and immediately launched into a pitch for the Sword and Plow organization, and what I could do as a member or operative. It was apparent he had accepted the facade that the Sword and Plow would have German support to fight the inevitable battle against the Bolsheviks and Red Army. There were also anti–Semitic overtones, but I was uncertain that Jerzy had bought into that as a legitimate issue. In any event, it was clear he was very proud of the organization, and what he saw as his leadership in it. I sat patiently and heard him out. I knew by instinct that if I were to accept recruitment, I would be trapped. He closed his argument by declaring, "We can do incredible things, so you must join us!" I cut him short, telling him pointedly that I was completely hostile to the idea. Jerzy shot back: "As a Rosinski, I would have expected more of you!" That stirred my anger. "Leave my family name out of this!" And that brought an end to Jerzy's efforts to win me over to the Sword and Plow.

I reported these developments to my superiors in the AK, which led to extended discussions as to how to handle this threat and eliminate or otherwise neutralize those we knew to be involved with the Gestapo. It was suggested that I join the Sword and Plow to report on its inner workings, but I flatly refused to do so. The AK intelligence network was able, over a period of several weeks, to learn through surveillance operations that three leaders of the Sword and Plow were traveling to Vienna for clandestine contacts with the Gestapo in that city. All three were Ph.D. academics.

This prompted the AK command to finally decide that all of them had to be eliminated, and done so in such a way as to send a message to the organization itself and, of more importance, the Gestapo in Warsaw.

The AK deferred to me and I issued the orders for their execution — but not against a stone wall. For the impact that was called for, and to minimize any security risks, all three were killed in public at the same hour and same day in mid–September 1943. I never carried a weapon, and consequently did not participate in the operation, other than being responsible for giving the order. I felt no remorse whatsoever for these traitors. However, I did have my qualms over Jerzy's involvement. He could easily have been among those targeted, but I was able to screen him from paying a penalty for his foolhardiness. After all, he was my good friend. Jerzy terminated his activities in the organization, but he did continue to work in the resistance in other ways. The Sword and Plow ceased to exist. To my knowledge, the German occupation abandoned any further efforts to create and run such organizations against the underground.

Soon after this episode with the Sword and Plow, another strange organization come to our attention that also had inevitable links to the Gestapo. In late winter of 1943, I received a call from a student and close friend, Janusz Medwadowski. Our families were also close socially. Janusz was a civil engineering student at the Warsaw Institute of Technology. He came right to the point of his call (but I wished he hadn't on the phone): "Jan, I'm positive you are with the AK. I know it's late to do this, but I want to join the AK and fight the Germans." "All right," I replied, "if that's what you want to do, I'll arrange a meeting this Sunday with some friends and we'll go from there."

That Sunday, our three-man team met first at my apartment, after which we walked the short distance to Janusz's apartment on the same street. After a series of questions about his background and intentions, he selected an AK code name and was sworn into the underground. Janusz looked ready to go to work. "Since I'm now a soldier, maybe you have an assignment for me?" he asked.

I replied, "The only thing you could do at the moment, is take my assignment to escort a Jewish family from Marszalkowska Street to a much safer house. We have received some information that their house may be under surveillance. So, here's what you do. Take this expensive book on architecture, to their apartment to return the book — that's your cover story. And that's what you should say, if anyone questions you. After all, you are a civil engineering student. Take the family to the house, where someone will be waiting for them."

Janusz turned up a scowl. "Well, I didn't know the AK is involved in helping Jews."

Rather than admonish him, I replied, "They are also Poles and they are in danger. We have to do something, they are being exterminated." Janusz took the book and memorized the two addresses where he would be going.

"Look for patrols," I cautioned. "Let them pass. Walk calmly, don't run. Whatever you do, don't attract unnecessary attention to yourself. It's now one o'clock, so you should be back here at your apartment by 2:30 P.M. We'll wait for you here."

Time passed: 3:00, then 4:00 and no sign of Janusz. Two of us decided to leave, and two remained, suspecting something may have gone wrong for this new recruit. At 5:00 P.M., we decided to check the first apartment where Janusz had gone to meet the family. However, just then the doorbell rang, and there was Janusz standing there, covered in blood. Some of his teeth were missing and it was obvious he had been badly beaten. I helped him wash up and waited for his story.

Janusz reported that he did everything as we instructed. Hardly able to talk with his damaged mouth, he explained that when he arrived at the door of the Jewish family's apartment, they were not there, but the Gestapo was. The Germans interrogated him, starting with, "What are you doing here?" Janusz said he told them his cover story about borrowing the book and stuck to it, despite the beating. Making no progress, the Gestapo officers took him to their headquarters on Aleja Szucha, where they again interrogated him. Finally, with Janusz holding to his cover story, they threw him in one of their cars and dumped him off in front of his apartment building.

At this point, Janusz was not to be trifled with. "This is it," he blurted. "I'm not going to risk my life to be involved in these kinds of operations. I want out of the AK." There was nothing we could do to convince him otherwise, so Janusz Medwadowski became an AK soldier with the shortest record of service — only a few hours. I told him how sorry I was, especially since I had told him to take my assignment. Had this not happened, it would have been me taken to Gestapo headquarters, not him.

Within our group, we remained puzzled, and not a little suspicious, as to how or why the Gestapo had released Janusz. So, I decided to seek help again from my mysterious Gestapo neighbor in our apartment building. I waited for him one evening on the stairway and finally met him. He invited me to his apartment, which was still sparsely furnished and absent signs of another person. I explained what had happened to Janusz, and our questioning his release by the Gestapo without extracting a confession. My contact agreed to look into the matter. He cautioned me not to try to contact him; he would contact me when he had information and we would meet only at his apartment. Ten days passed before he finally came to my apartment and invited me to join him.

The first thing he said when we sat down was, "The Jewish family in question had confided in the Gestapo that the AK intended to help them move to a safer place to live." I was dumbstruck with disbelief. I immediately thought of my family's own security. We had been hiding a Jewish man — I don't recall his name — at our Black Creek estate for nearly two years, so far without incident. If the Gestapo could reach him, we would be in serious straits. For all this time we had been ignoring the occupation order that anyone harboring or aiding Jews would be sentenced to death. I found myself sitting there almost paralyzed. I did not want to believe this could be true. Finally I asked him the remaining important question: "How could Janusz have been released after his arrest and the occupation order?"

"Well," my neighbor replied, "it appears he was very lucky that his father was a general in the Polish artillery. There seems to be a soft spot in the minds of all military officers, including Germans, even for enemy officers. In any event, he was very lucky to have gotten out alive." As he was talking, I noticed his Polish was perfect, so I thought he might have given his loyalty to Germany and the Gestapo, even before the war. That still did not answer what had motivated him to approach me with an offer to be of assistance in a pinch. He chatted some more about events on the Eastern Front and the increasingly high losses of men and weaponry. He thought that Germany likely would not recover from the invasion of the Soviet Union. Perhaps it was this perceived fate that had prompted him to approach me.

After I returned to my apartment, I was in a quandary as to what should be done about the Jewish man we were hiding at the estate. In any event, this situation prompted me to call a meeting of our group the next day and report what I had learned — that Janusz had gone directly into a trap. So, I asked them, "What shall we do now?" There were eight of us at the meeting. Some advised we should cease all aid activity. I called my uncle Jan and asked for his advice. He told me, "Anyone with a gun to his head will do what is demanded. I know you wouldn't, but there are others who would sell out their own family for a dollar, just to save their lives."

So the meeting of eight reached the simple conclusion that we must spread a warning within the AK of this betrayal. I advised consideration of further options and said we should take no sudden actions we would later regret. "Let's discuss this again and again," I suggested. This is how our meeting ended. No words could describe our emotions about this very disturbing situation. Later, I informed the group about what I had learned about the Eastern Front from my Gestapo contact.

The only way we could ever determine or uncover the myriad of ways the Gestapo penetrated Polish society was literally to run into them in the course of our underground operations, or receive intelligence from within the AK on specific Gestapo activities. Not long after this setback, five of our group's "conspirators" met to discuss information one of our members had reported on a Polish man who was cooperating with the Gestapo for reward. He owned a small confectionery shop near the square and monument of Nikolaus Kopernicus. I volunteered to pay him a visit the following Saturday morning. No one seemed to object, so my task was set.

As I entered the shop that morning, I could see that the owner looked to be reasonably prosperous, and perhaps more so, from just selling candies. Just before going in, I noticed two men across the street, facing toward the shop, reading newspapers, while two other men were at a nearby bus stop. Adding to this interesting and suspicious scene was a German soldier, with slung rifle, walking around the monument. This was enough to kick off my internal alarm system, but somehow I didn't read this as a real security threat. I noticed that the owner also was keeping an eye on the street scene from his shop window.

When the owner asked what I cared to buy, I replied, "Well, I'm not here to buy anything. I came only to talk to you. We have been informed that you are handing over some people to the Germans. Now, I'll tell you something — these people are human beings. No matter how you look at them, they are as us. Therefore, we cannot permit you to continue selling anyone to our enemy. If you will not stop these treacherous acts, we will blow this place to kingdom come, with you in it. So, I suggest you think it over. I may or may not stop by again to talk to you. As you know me, I'd prefer not to come again. My suggestion is simply, why don't you stop doing these things." As I opened the door to go out, I waved to the two men across the street reading their newspapers and, surprisingly, they waved back. Also, just then the other two men at the bus stop started to walk away. I noticed that the owner had not missed any of this, and probably came to the conclusion that I had a team backing me up. Frankly, I couldn't have scripted it any better if I'd been a movie director. I felt brave enough to give the shopkeeper a final admonishment: "It's up to you, so we will see now what happens!"

At our next meeting, I reported on my Saturday morning at the confectionery shop. Needless to say, I had their full and abiding attention. In amazement, they all asked at once if I had any connection with the men on the street. I laughed and told them I'd never seen them before in my life, and had never talked to them. Then we all had a laugh. Fortunately, I never returned to the shop. We did detect a notable lessening of his activities. The man's fate was not known, but it is likely he did not survive long after the war, if even then.

Beyond the underground's constant concerns over Gestapo activities throughout the country, there was also the presence in Warsaw of the "storm troops," or SA (*Sturmabteilung*). The SA was a paramilitary organization of the National Socialist German Workers Party, or the Nazi Party. It was commonly referred to as the "Brown Shirts" for the brownish tan uniforms. It had its beginning in Germany in the early 1920s and a stormy history thereafter. Fortunately, I was never involved with, or set against, the SA, and I do not recall specific AK operations directed against the SA element in Warsaw. However, I learned of a bizarre incident that reflects the incredible determination of one man to exact his own brand of revenge on the SA commander, or *Gauleiter*, in Warsaw.

I was acquainted with a gentleman, Stanislaw Janiszeski, who worked for my two uncles at various jobs. He was an accomplished outdoorsman and I joined him on two occasions on treks into the Tatra Mountains. Stanislaw had a good friend who spoke fluent German and passable Polish. I met him occasionally in Stanislaw's company and, in the course of our conversations, I suspected him to be German. One day, this fellow invited me to join him in a visit to the SA headquarters in Warsaw. I should add here that, to this day, I don't recall why I would have exposed myself unnecessarily to these known party goons, but for some reason I accepted the invitation. Stanislaw introduced me to the gauleiter, whose name I do not remember. The gauleiter asked me what I was doing, so I showed him my forged ID papers and explained my work as a contract supplier of food goods to the German army. He immediately reached for the phone and called to what I believe was the Gestapo and verified my status. While he was doing that, some other SA officers asked, "Why are you working for us?" "Well, simply put," I replied, "you won the war, so I'm working for you. If we had won the war, you would be working for me." That elementary logic seemed to satisfy them, and even the gauleiter remarked, "Yes, that's probably right." This is all that I can recall of our visit, and my only contact with the SA. Certainly, it would be my only meeting with the gauleiter, for his life would soon be cut short.

A few days after our visit, I saw Stanislaw's friend wearing an official-appearing suit made of the same brown material as the SA uniforms. There appeared to be no insignias or an Iron Cross, but it was close in style to their uniforms. I set this aside mentally, until soon thereafter I saw him again riding a BMW motorcycle similar to the model used by the German army. This seemed to confirm, in my mind, that the fellow was German. I saw him a few more times, riding in the streets, but I did not talk to him. Now, the remainder of this story comes from my uncle Stanislaw. What I learned was that this rather strange man had ridden his motorcycle to SA headquarters, past the outer guard post, and walked boldly into the building. He barged into the gauleiter's office, pulled out a pistol and killed the gauleiter with shots to his head. When the secretary burst through the door, he shot her as well. He then yelled out something to the effect that "the killer is escaping" and began shooting through a rear door off the office that led to an outside courtyard and the rear of the building. SA men raced into the office, took in the scene and assumed the actual killer had escaped out the back. They rushed out the door, continuing their pursuit, which was headed to nowhere.

Our man, the assassin, holstered his pistol, calmly walked out of the headquarters, mounted his BMW, gave a "Heil Hitler" salute, and rode out the gate past the guard post. He rode to a nearby house where he had stashed a change of clothes, parked and covered the motorcycle, then hopped on a bicycle for the rest of his escape. As he rode down a street toward the Vistula River, a German patrol crossed his path. The squad leader asked whether "our man" had seen anyone on a motorcycle. He told them he had just spotted a motorcycle heading up the road alongside the river, at which point the patrol turned around, tires squealing, and sped off. The assassin then calmly rode his bicycle into obscurity.

I remain convinced this man was a German who must have had good reason to kill the SA commander. The action obviously was well planned and carried out flawlessly. I'm certain his disappearance was also expertly executed. In the aftermath of this incident, I was unable to determine the number or identities of the Poles who were executed in reprisal for this assassination. Tragically, the toll was extremely heavy.

CHAPTER 7

Barbarity

Looking back on the morning of the German invasion as I was leaving by train from Katowice for Warsaw, there was no way I could have prepared or steeled myself for the horrors visited on the people of Poland for nearly six years of the occupation. The Stuka dive bomber attacks on the civilian passenger train were an abrupt reminder that suddenly we were at war, but this was not yet personal. We had not yet looked the enemy in the eye to see a country and its soldiers conducting a war outside the boundaries of all norms of human civilization. Worse yet, we also could not yet see the Bolsheviks and Red Army waiting in the wings to exact their own brand of conquest and control over a subjugated people.

Not long into the occupation, a myth of sorts arose pointing to the Gestapo and SS units as the perpetrators of atrocities, not the regular army. Just before the attack on Poland was launched, Hitler had told his generals at the conference on the Obersalzberg on August 22 that things would happen "which would not be to the taste of German generals," and he warned them that they "should not interfere in such matters but restrict themselves to their military duties" (Shirer, p. 660).

Whether it was a lack of military discipline at a small unit level or also in higher command elements, the regular army soon joined in delivering harsh treatment to the civilian Polish population, especially in Warsaw. Soon after giving my oath to the AK in mid-winter 1940, I observed an incident while walking along Marszalkowska Street. A squad or patrol of what appeared to be regular German troops were marching toward me when they came upon two young Polish boys, ages about 10 to 12 years. The patrol leader stopped the squad just as the boys were passing. It looked as though he was attempting to talk to them. Suddenly, one of the soldiers grabbed one boy and kicked him viciously. Then he grabbed him again by the legs and crushed him into a cement wall, killing him instantly. The other boy was able to run away down a side street and save himself. Another almost similar incident occurred in the city center. Again it was two Polish boys who were ill fated to be confronted by an army patrol. One was shot and the other beaten. I was able to get a bucket of water to help the one boy to clean his wounds, but I could not stay any longer for fear that the patrol might double back to where we were. In this latter incident, there were several people on the street who witnessed the atrocity. You could see them, particularly men, stop on the sidewalk and turn their look of total hatred toward the soldiers. It became obvious the soldiers could sense the mounting hostility, as they quickly marched away. It was such incidents of mindless brutality that strengthened those of us in the underground to fight back however we could.

From late 1941 into 1942, the Germans were systematically arresting Poles to fill their labor camps in Germany. The roundups could happen at any place at any hour of the day or night. What was occurring on the streets created constant pressure to acquire a sense of awareness of what was happening around you. Your only defense was to develop almost the instincts of a hunted animal. It is hard to imagine, but at times the frequency and intensity of these roundups began to concern even German officials. As one such person wrote to Governor Frank, "The wild and ruthless man hunt, as exercised everywhere in towns and country, in streets and squares, stations, even in churches, at night in homes, has badly shaken the feeling of security of the inhabitants. Everybody is exposed to the danger of being seized anywhere and at any time by the police, suddenly and unexpectedly, and of being sent to an assembly camp. No one knows what has happened to them" (Shirer, pp. 947–948). They just didn't come home again.

By 1942, both SS and regular army units began random shootings of Poles in the streets, frequently not bothering to arrest anyone. One afternoon as I was walking a block off Marszalkowska Street, a troop truck pulled up to the side of the street immediately behind me. Several soldiers jumped out from the back of the truck as a young SS officer emerged from the truck cab. The dual silver lightning bolts on his uniform collar was all that was needed to raise a crashing alarm in my mind. He commanded the soldiers to round up 10 people—whoever were the closest to grab— and lined them up against a wall. I was just a few steps farther away from those forced to the wall, or perhaps I was lucky enough to be ignored. But I was not yet able to escape his attention. He turned and strode forcefully over to me, drew his pistol, put it to my head, and blurted out with rancid breath, "Watch this, and if you make a sound, I'll pull the trigger."

The soldiers then shot all ten persons, men and women. Blood splattered on the wall, and pools of blood began to cover the walkway where the crumpled bodies lay. I was still breaking out in a cold sweat as the officer ordered his men back into the truck and then pulled away from the assassination scene. Not a word was spoken other than that one order. The officer glanced at me as he got into the truck, perhaps thinking he would come back and shoot me as well, or conversely, allow me to live another day. These are moments that can cripple anyone for life, physically or mentally. Mostly, the mind cannot assemble rational thought, but the shocking thought does come through that *here is where my life ends*. The incident happened so swiftly that others on the street seemed to freeze in place. People were afraid to approach the bodies, but a few found some flowers and spread them over the dead. When confronted with such vile acts, most Poles, including family members, were afraid to come and claim the bodies. It was not uncommon for the dead to lie unclaimed for days, until the smell of human decay finally prompted laborers to remove them for burial. So families waited in vain for loved ones — mothers, fathers — to come home. I knew that would be the case in this incident, so not having been selected to join them in death, I could not allow these tragic souls to lie there into the night and days ahead. Later that evening I recruited and paid two teenage boys to go to the killing site and remove whatever identification they could find on the bodies and bring them to me. I then sent others in my group to the addresses noted in the documents to report the tragic news. Another of many unpleasant tasks of survival.

Some could not stand idly by and took revenge in a moment of desperation. Such was an incident I observed on another street when a Polish fellow dashed out of a gate and into the street, pistol drawn, just as a German staff car was passing by. The passenger in the rear seat appeared to be a senior officer. The man fired into the car. The driver stopped as they returned fire. The assailant was able to escape down a side street, leaving the car to continue on its way. Perhaps all lived for another day.

On one of my "business" trips across the Vistula River to the district of Praga, I saw that a streetcar had been stopped by regular German army troops. They forced five Poles, both men and women, into the street and photographed them one at a time as they were being shot. After executing all five, they marched on, laughing and joking as they took their last pictures. As usual, the dead were left to the attentions of those witnessing the atrocity, so that bodies could be identified and somehow families contacted.

Mindless killing, even of a single person, was sometimes almost too much to bear. A kindly peasant farmer who was a member of the AK would occasionally slaughter a pig or cow and deliver meat cuts — all illegal of course — to my family and others in Warsaw. We were so appreciative of his supply, which was our only source of any meat. However, when he did not appear for more than a month, we began to look for him. We discovered that a German patrol had stopped him at a checkpoint, discovered the meat carefully covered in his horse-drawn wagon and shot him on the spot. They left his body on the road, with the horse wagon standing there hours later. His name was Twardowski, and he is remembered.

Then we learned that German patrols were starting to pick up Polish children, but only those of light complexion, blond hair and blue eyes. In at least one Nazi document, such children were referred to as "racially valuable elements." They were being transported to Germany where they would be raised as Germans. Here again, there was little the AK could do about it, particularly since it was conducted randomly. I learned that the AK command sent a report on this development to the exile government in London for the attention of President Roosevelt. Sometime later, we learned that the report had been received with skepticism. For this and other reasons, our short-term judgment was that we would best concentrate our efforts with the British, especially since they had an excellent intelligence service with operations in Poland, as well as ties to the underground command. So, even in our small group, we decided, "Let's work with them."

The events of 1942 could not pass without those of us in the underground being increasingly aware of Hitler's persecution of Jews. The policies toward Jews in the Third Reich were soon being duplicated in Poland. At two successive meetings of our group, we decided we must do something to help. I was chosen to seek out and form a cooperative effort with a rabbi, who surprisingly appeared to be living openly in Warsaw, as was his congregation. After taking some time to locate his residence, I appeared at his door unannounced and introduced myself, omitting any reference to the AK. I told him that we could not stand silently by while Polish Jews were being persecuted and killed. I ended my offer by stating, "You are the target of the German occupation — they will kill you before others, so we are here to help." He appeared unsettled and cautious at my offer, perhaps wondering if it was a provocation. Unfortunately, it became futile to continue talking to him, so I abruptly turned and walked away. Three days later, at our group meeting, I reported my meeting with the rabbi, which news was received with disappointment. The typical reaction was, "This is hard to believe." I only told them to go ahead and meet the rabbi and find out for themselves. "For me," I said, "I'll look elsewhere. Just leave it alone. Let's talk to some others." This ended this sad and puzzling episode.

Not long after my encounter with the rabbi, I saw some stolen SS photos of a roundup of some 2,000 Jews in Warsaw. They were being loaded into boxcars of trains under SS guard. But, on closer look, there appeared to be only two guards, each holding dogs on leashes. Everyone — women, men and children — were moving to the boxcars peacefully and without apparent incident. We should have been doing something to help. However, what struck me was their willingness to go without protest or fighting back. I thought that, if they had resisted, perhaps 100 persons might have been shot, but most might have had a chance to escape. We should have been ready for that. As it turned out, all were condemned in death camps.

The early warnings were there for all to see. Early in the occupation a curfew was imposed on Jews — 8:00 P.M. in winter and 9:00 P.M. in summer. An order in late November 1939 compelled all Jews to wear a yellow Star of David where it could be seen. That brought to mind an incident soon after that order was issued. Walking a short distance from my apartment, I saw three young Jewish men walking toward me from a side street. All three were wearing the yellow star. Unseen by them was a German patrol of three men approaching from a different direction. Seeing a convergence coming, I called out to warn them to get off the street. The men ignored my alert, as one of them called back to me, "No, there is nothing they can do to us." With that, I dodged into the nearest house and asked and received a few moments of refuge. I could see from a window the soldiers stopping the men. They were thrown to the ground and viciously kicked, but left alive, as the soldiers laughed and made their way down the street. I took some water out to them so they could clean their wounds. The only thing I could say to them was, "Why don't you wash yourselves, and next time stay out of the way." They were fortunate not to have been arrested.

Yet another horrific experience was to surface — this one visited on Dr. Barbara Natorff-Tokarczyk, my future fiancée and wife. She related this to me while I was at the Maltanski Hospital being treated for a shallow wound from a bullet that had ricocheted into my underarm. It was the summer of 1941. Barbara's father, a wealthy industrialist, had purchased a small villa where Barbara could study quietly for her medical courses. She would also invite friends to stay with her from time to time. It was situated on a stream with a sandy shoreline that flowed into the River Wisla and was near the village of Falenica and the town of Otwock. An otherwise peaceful afternoon was abruptly interrupted by the arrival of a German army convoy that cut across the villa's land and stopped alongside the river. Barbara said she took a pair of binoculars and went up to the roof for a better view of what was happening. There she observed possibly as many as 100 Jews being off-loaded from the trucks. Standing there helplessly, they were quickly surrounded by armed soldiers. A mounted machine gun was uncovered on one truck and began firing at the captives, while other soldiers followed suit with their machine pistols. The firing didn't stop until bodies were thrown all along the sandy riverbank. Then a bulldozer was off-loaded from a trailer and a large trench dug in the sand. The bodies of the Jews were then bulldozed into the trench and covered. The convoy packed up and departed the way they came.

Barbara remarked that unfortunately she had no camera with her, so she was unable to photograph this atrocity. However, she thought she saw some movement in the sand, so she rushed off the roof and ran to the burial site. Having no shovel, she started digging in the sand with her hands, hopefully looking for someone still alive. By this time, all had suffocated, and it was also too difficult for her to pull any of the bodies out of the sand. There was nothing I could say or do that would erase this scene of horror from her memory. At a loss for words, I could only manage to say, "It looks like this terror will go on and never stop." Little did I know that my own horror experience — more than what I had already endured — was soon to come.

Psychological terror was also being thrown at the Polish people. The Gestapo would post a list on a street kiosk of Poles to be shot the next day. On one kiosk, I saw the name of a close friend whose father headed a tax administration office for tobacco and alcohol. Their family name, as I recall, was Borkowski. When I returned home and told my mother about the executions, she said, "Why don't you call his father to see what could be done?" This seemed like a worthwhile suggestion, so I called and my friend answered the phone. "You're alive!" I exclaimed. "Aren't you in German hands?" "No," he replied. "What happened was my wallet was stolen, and the Germans must have arrested the thief, who got my identity as well as my money." "Well, I wanted to talk to your father," I told him, "but obviously that is no longer necessary. So, congratulations, you are still among the living." This was another persecution that passed under the German heel.

These posted names became very demoralizing, for we would know, or read, who would be killed the next day. Some lists contained 20 or more names and some only 10, but that was at only one kiosk. All this was very hard to accept, especially since these killings would be carried out on the street. Poles were simply lined up in front of a building or wall and shot. That was it! The execution sites were picked at random, and those who happened to be passing by were stopped and forced to watch these horrible scenes. This occurred all over Warsaw. After the shootings, some people would come and put flowers over the bloodied street. So, this is what we confronted every day. The AK could hardly exist under these circumstances. The hatred of the Germans intensified to the boiling point. Many came to believe that this was the starting point for the national uprising. Personally, I believe that the impetus for the uprising came from the exiled Polish government in London. The actual signal to launch the uprising was a BBC broadcast of an intentional error in a Chopin work or melody. The commander-in-chief of the Polish Underground Army (AK) and the Warsaw Uprising, General Tadeusz "Bor" Komorowski gave the order, but the authority came from London. I don't know the details, and because of the loss of my eyesight, I cannot read about this crucial time in Polish history. Nevertheless, I remain critical, even today, of the decision to launch the uprising.

One afternoon in late September 1943, I noted a feature article in the German *Völkischer Beobachter* that SS Brigadeführer (Major General) Franz Kutschera was being transferred to Poland to "clean up the situation in Warsaw." He had earned the dishonorable title of the "Butcher of the Balkans," so this could only mean the worst for all Poles in the city. True to his reputation, Kutzchera's presence in the capital was immediately felt through reinvigorated SS and Gestapo operations against the underground and population in general. It was for this reason that I began to reduce the time I spent on the street, especially during the day. Kutchera was an Austrian who had served as a boy in the Austro-Hungarian navy, had studied in Budapest, and had lived in Czechoslovakia. So he was an East European expert. Joining the Nazi party in 1930, he was an early enthusiast who by the age of thirty-four was gauleiter of his native Carinthia. After front line service in France, he found his metier in the grisly business of keeping order in the east. He served successfully as "SS and Police Chief" in Russland Mitte and in Mogilev. Warsaw was no doubt a worthy promotion (Davies, p. 89).

Toward the end of that winter of 1943-1944, my AK group became aware that a very sensitive and important operation was being planned. We did not know of any details, other than it would be an attack. Again, it was better not to be overly curious unless you were called on or ordered into action. Ignoring my own caution to stay off the streets, I came close to crossing the path of this awaited AK action on the morning of February 1, 1944. Less than a block away, off Aleje Ujazdowskie, intense firing broke out — sounds of German machine guns and other weapons, including hand grenades, carried by the AK. I broke out in a run of Olympic performance away from the clash, down Piekna Street. I sought refuge in the nearby Poroski horse stables. So until the next morning I hid out in a horse stall, one I fortunately did not have to share with a horse. What had sent me fleeing, I was soon to learn, was the AK assassination of Franz Kutschera.

The plan to kill Kutschera originated in the AK's K-Division Command. The eight assassins were chosen from 1st Platoon of the Pegasus organization. The leader was (code name) Cpl. "Flight." The time was the morning of 1 February 1944. The place was the beautiful Aleje Ujazdowskie near the park-side junction of Chopen Street. Kutschera's steel-gray Opel Admiral sedan turned onto the boulevard, past the former British Embassy at 9:06 A.M. It was followed by an open truck filled with soldiers. Armed SS men marched alongside. As it traveled slowly north, its arrival was signaled by a woman on the roadside who pulled up the hood of her coat and crossed the street. After perhaps 150 yards, a car roared around the corner of Pius XI Street, careened onto the wrong side of the road, and smashed head-on into Kutschera's convoy. Almost immediately, Flight ran down the right-hand pavement and emptied his Sten gun at point-blank range through the Opel's open window. An accomplice arrived on the other side and repeated the performance. Kutschera was already dying. A volley of German machine-gun fire felled two attackers, but a fierce hail of bullets and grenades from friends posted nearby kept the enemy at bay while the wounded were picked up and the whole team scrambled into two waiting cars. At 9:08 A.M. both cars escaped. One of them later ran into a German checkpoint on one of the Vistula bridges, and the occupants had to jump over the balustrade into the freezing river. The other made it to the Old Town, where it met a physician, "Dr. Max," but then toured the hospitals, searching desperately for a specialist surgeon who dared attend Flight's wounds. The operations were performed late at night. Both patients deteriorated. Their mothers were summoned before they died. Flight was given a death certificate naming tuberculosis of the liver, and he was buried in the city cemetery by a regular undertaker (Davies, pp. 197–198).

During the night in the stable, I made my way to the adjoining building where the stable owner, Poroski, kept an apartment. After some searching, I found a pistol in a chest drawer and slipped it into my pocket. I cannot recall now whether I took it with or without Poroski's permission. The next morning I set out for home, but then I came upon a large German guard contingent in front of a building on Piekna Street. I wanted to avoid being stopped and subjected to a body search, so I quickly reversed my walk and returned to the Poroski apartment to put the gun back where I had found it. I finally made it back to my apartment without incident. However, that was not to be the end of events connected to the assassination of Kutschera. Revenge exacted by the SS and Gestapo was soon to follow.

A week later, ignoring my own caution on street exposure, I was swept up by three SS officers in a sedan car. The car, traveling at a higher speed and quieter than a truck, caught me completely unaware. I was taken to Gestapo headquarters on Aleja Szucha and deposited in a holding room. Thirty minutes later, without being questioned or interrogated, I was released. However, fate struck again, as I was grabbed the next day and taken by truck with others for what would be a burial detail. We were taken to an open area by the King's Garden, at a place known as Lazienki near the public baths. I was horrified to see bodies piled in large numbers in this open field. There appeared to be about 100 of us who were given shovels and ordered to start digging graves. It was impossible to count the bodies.

All I know — and will never forget — is that it took all of us three long days to dig a mass grave and bury these poor souls. Some of the SS guards had taken three young Jewish women, raped them and shot them at the burial site. For some reason, I attracted the attention of one guard, who ordered me to bury the women. I would have tried to search the bodies for any identification, so I could inform their families, but that was impossible under the close watch of the guards. I and the other captive laborers were forced to sleep on the ground and subsist on bread and dirty water for the three days. By the end of this ordeal, I had convinced myself that we would also all be shot after this devil's detail was finished. Miraculously, we were allowed to go. Some of the laborers were so emotionally affected by the ordeal that they wandered off aimlessly. Cloaked in the smell of death that seemed to stay with me, I made my way home to a hysterical mother who had feared the worse but could hardly imagine what actually had happened to me. According to information within the AK command, nearly 5,000 Poles were killed in reprisal for the Kutschera assassination.

In the weeks prior to the uprising in the Jewish ghetto in Warsaw in April 1943 our group sought some way we could help those brave people who would soon be fighting for their lives. It was virtually impossible to provide weapons. In what I recall to be the only allied airdrop over the city that included weapons and ammunition, half landed in German hands and half in Polish. Much of the ammunition was useless because there were few matches to the weapons. Nearly a year before the uprising the AK command set up a clandestine organization, known by its code name of "Zegota." It soon made its mark in the rescue of Jewish children, placing them in safekeeping through churches and trusted underground elements. We were not involved in that effort, but we stood ready to help if called on. Meanwhile, I finally came up with a modest scheme to supply bread to those trapped in the ghetto. We were baking some bread in our apartment, but a somewhat larger baking operation was started in the watchman's cabin at our Black Creek estate. The watchman and his wife and son were involved, and it was overseen by my aunt Zofia. We were able to smuggle most of the bread into Warsaw on a narrow-gauge railway that was not closely watched by the Germans. We would hide the bread on the train while it was at Czarna Struga station, which was not far from the estate, and then it would be retrieved by someone in our group on arrival in Warsaw.

We would place some loaves of bread in a bag and tie a string or small rope to the bag and then toss the bag in a circle and whip it up and over the wall of the ghetto. We did this on Zlota Street and two other streets that ran alongside the walls of the ghetto. Our first efforts bounced the bread off the wall, but then our technique improved. We had to move fast to avoid German guards on the street. In a month of this activity, we were fired on several times, but the soldiers didn't seem stirred up enough to chase after us. We usually took the electric tram car to and from the ghetto area. We also used another technique when the elevated tram was passing above and alongside the ghetto walls. We could then sling the package of bread out the tram window and over the walls. This occasionally drew gunfire, with the bullets shattering glass and ricocheting inside the car. It was amazing that no one in our group was arrested or shot. But the risk eventually became too high, so after one month we were forced to discontinue the bread supply operation.

By 1943 I was spending nearly half of each day forging German documents, which included ID cards, travel papers, and work permits. Not wanting to risk using my mother's apartment, I was able to be alone in a small apartment owned by the family on Kozia Street in the Old Town. It took a great deal of concentration to detail, filling in the forms by hand or with an ancient, but good, working German typewriter. This was not a mass-production operation. Often it would take a full day to complete a set of documents, error free. The forms were genuine and procured clandestinely by the AK supply network, usually by my own efforts. The secret was to enter a German administrative office without drawing attention and quickly scan a clerk's desk for a stack of forms. Forging signatures took a great deal of care and was usually done with a quick scribbling motion, rather than in a laborious style. This reflected the human tendency of officials who signed hundreds of documents to write their signatures quickly and often in a sloppy manner. Mistakes that I made on any form had to be immediately destroyed, so I was burning these papers in the apartment's fireplace. My family became suspicious of what I was up to, but nothing was spoken among us. Again, that old rule for confidentiality.

In the few weeks before the Ghetto Uprising in April 1943 an increasing number of documents I was forging were for Jews, who were risking escaping to the outside world. I could only hope that they served their purpose. Occasionally, I would receive some feedback from the AK about their usefulness. My own forged documents held up well throughout the occupation, with that one near exception one afternoon on the ski slopes of the Tatra Mountains. The AK helped protect my forgery activity by searching for and providing vacant apartments where I could move my supplies. Some were unclean or unkempt, but still contained basic furniture. These moves would be made every few weeks as a precaution against unwanted attention. One of my "tools" was a pair of binoculars that I would use to survey the street before setting out from whatever apartment I was using. I had a pocket sown on the inside of my pants where I kept the binoculars, ever ready to use them when needed.

The Ghetto Uprising affected us deeply, but there was little we could do, particularly when a large German SS and police force moved in to torch the ghetto. By mid–May the resistance had been crushed. The German troops were under the command of SS-Brigadeführer Jürgen Stroop. I knew nothing of this man, of course, but fate would later put me in his presence in a most unusual place and situation. One can read about the Ghetto Uprising from many sources. Stroop's report is full of reluctant admiration for his adversaries: "Jews and Jewesses shot from two pistols at the same time.... Jewesses carried loaded [weapons] in their clothing.... At the last moment, they would pull out hand grenades ... and throw them at the soldiers" (Davies, p. 202).

April 1943 would bring more tragedy to Poland, but this time from the east. On the afternoon of April 11, as I was passing an intersection near our apartment, a German radio news report was broadcast on one of many speakers positioned over the streets of the city. Berlin announced the discovery of a mass grave near the Ukraine town of Smolensk containing the bodies of 4,231 Polish officers. At first we didn't know what to make of it. Was this German propaganda placing the blame on the Red Army, or were they covering up their own atrocity? One fact was certain. Thousands of Polish families had not heard of the fate of their husbands and sons since their disappearance during the Soviet invasion of Poland launched on September 17, 1939. My family fortunately was not affected, but we knew many families that were. As investigations unfolded, Soviet guilt was eventually established, not only for this atrocity but also in other POW camps where Polish army personnel were held. It would not be until 1990 that Moscow finally admitted to the killings by the NKVD. There are certain acts in life that cannot be overlooked or forgiven. From that day on my hatred for the Soviet state and Russian communists has remained unabated.

Yet, it was not until many years later, when I began to think of recording my wartime experiences, that I learned of the considerable internal disputes within the German high command over the mounting atrocities committed by the SS and Gestapo against the Polish people. By some accounts, there were more than a handful of generals and senior staff officers who risked their careers in opposition to Hitler's policies of extermination of Polish Jews, intelligentsia, landowners and clergy. One such officer who came to my attention was Colonel General Johannes von Blaskowitz. Born in East Prussia to a religious family — his father was a Lutheran pastor — Blaskowitz carried into his military career a strong sense of moral responsibility in his command. After commanding the German 8th Army, which spearheaded the attack on Warsaw, he became the military governor of Poland. Much to his frustration, however, his real authority was virtually suborned to Governor-General Hans Frank. This was no impediment to the general, as he wrote several memoranda and letters to the army high command about the uncontrolled actions of the SS, Gestapo and Einsatz Gruppen. The army commander-in-chief, Field Marshal Walter von Brauchitsch was a principal recipient of these communications, with some copies also reaching Hitler or at least the contents brought to his attention.

An enraged Fuehrer responded by twice relieving Blaskowitz of his command, as well as blocking his promotion to field marshal. Tensions mounted in several instances through early 1940 between the army and the SS, but in the end Hitler, with Goering and Himmler, would have his way. What many army commanders were sensitive to was the impact that the atrocities had on the morale of army troops and the undercutting of discipline. In fact, this was soon seen on the streets of Warsaw.

Blaskowitz, holding an occupation command in France at the end of the war, was arrested and sent to Nuremberg for trial on war crime charges. Never thought by Allied prosecutors to face any serious sentence, he nevertheless committed suicide in 1948 as his trial opened (Giziowski).

CHAPTER 8

The Deserter

In the fall of 1943 I traveled again to the mountain resort town of Zakopane to meet secretly with the AK group there, and also to remove myself from the daily pressures of surviving in Warsaw. It was a beautiful time of year in the Tatras, which recharged my batteries for the winter to come. Since the mountain range straddled Poland and Czechoslovakia, we used both clandestine crossing points and official border crossings to occasionally smuggle Poles across to wherever their destinations might be, including onward underground routes to London. AK elements also operated in Czechoslovakia, so many or most of those who were sent through the underground remained in our hands.

The afternoon after my arrival in Zakopane, I went to my favorite restaurant for a midday meal attended to by the owner, with whom I was well acquainted. There were some German soldiers there, presumably on a short-term leave. I didn't want to draw attention to myself, so I took a table in a rear corner of the restaurant. As an avid fisherman, when I couldn't catch fish I would order it. I placed my order with the owner for a bowl of chicken soup and two fried trout. When I was served, my fare drew unintended but immediate attention from the soldiers sitting close to the front of the restaurant. Soon, a young officer, I believe a lieutenant, approached my table. He had an inhospitable look about him, so it appeared we would not be having a social conversation. His complaint was food — mine, exactly. He wanted me to know he was offended that I was enjoying a fine meal while he and his fellow soldiers were by regulation compelled to eat only a common *eintopfgericht*, or German stew. I knew it to be true about his complaint, as the army command had issued orders that soldiers were to confine their diet to this dish and that public eateries were likewise compelled to offer only the stew to German army personnel.

Initially, I think he was somewhat taken aback that I could respond in acceptable German. This made him pause for a moment. Then I explained: "Well, you see I was able to catch these trout and I had asked the owner to prepare them for me."

I invited him to join me, which evoked a subdued response. He quieted down and we continued to chat. After introducing ourselves, he explained that he was a student of art and architecture. I surmised we were about the same age, perhaps he being a year or two older. An idea suddenly came to mind, and I asked the owner to give me a new white tablecloth. I asked my guest what his specialty or primary interest in art was, and he replied that it was charcoal drawings, especially now since he could carry no art supplies with him. I then invited him to make a drawing on the tablecloth. He smiled, as I think he saw this as a challenge, and retrieved a piece of charcoal from his kit. Then he seemed hesitant to blacken the tablecloth, but I told him to please go ahead and draw something. I suggested a portrait of a woman, and possibly a castle.

After about thirty minutes, his first drawing of a young woman gradually became clearer. The detail and flair were astounding. I could not believe my eyes; it was truly magnificent! I touched his arm, exclaiming, "You know, you must be another Dürer!" I was referring to perhaps the greatest German renaissance painter, Albrecht Dürer, a native of Nuremberg, who may be best known for his prints. As the soldier added the finishing touches to the drawing, I asked him if he might have been acquainted with the woman he had just drawn. He smiled, as he replied, "No, unfortunately, I have her face only in my memory from the front cover of a Parisian magazine, but she was a Polish girl. I fell in love with that face, so it was easy for me to bring her image to mind." Well, I didn't want to admit it to him, but at least in my dreams, she was the one I had hoped to marry. She was a student at Warsaw University, and I'm sure the center of many other young men's fantasies. The fact that I now had a portrait of her almost brought tears to my eyes. Unfortunately, she was unable to finish her studies due to a life-threatening illness. I visited her once at a sanitarium in Otwock, a small town near Warsaw. On a second visit, I was told by the staff that she had died. I asked him to please finish the drawing, which he did. I told the owner I would pay for the tablecloth, if he would wrap it so that I could take it with me.

Having put the last touches to the drawing, the soldier turned to me and asked, "Will you be here tomorrow?" "Yes," I said. "I will be here for dinner, but a little early at about 5:00 P.M. Why don't you come at six o'clock. You will find me at a table in the back corner. We can then chat about anything you like." I then asked the owner to fry two trout for my new artist friend. This of course, was a delicacy, especially in wartime, as he well knew.

The next day, he came as I had suggested, and started to order the standard dish of *Eintopfgericht*. I told him to set that aside and join me for a dinner of fried trout. To avoid embarrassing him, I told him that I had caught four trout the previous day and wanted to share my luck on a favorite stream not far away. He was ecstatic and began to chat in animated fashion. Then suddenly he turned serious, as he informed me he had been ordered to the Eastern Front with his division. "For me," he lamented, "this is certain death. I will not survive." As he paused, there was a moment when neither one of us spoke. Finally, he said what was really on his mind. Avoiding eye contact, he asked, "Could you possibly help me somehow?"

"How could I help?" I asked. "I'm here just for two more days, then I must return to Warsaw and my work." He replied, "Well, can you help me to desert. I want to just disappear."

Jan's best friend and fellow AK operative, Zosia Gasienica-Gladczan, in the Tatra Mountains, 1937.

My first reaction was that this might be a provocation, a trap ending in my arrest by the Gestapo. Thinking on, I concluded he must be sincere, that it was not a provocation. So, I decided to take the risk. Actually, what prompted me to do so was the news we were hearing about the gradual withdrawal westward of major German forces in the aftermath of the surrender of the German Sixth Army at Stalingrad. Added to that, of course, was the British defeat of the Afrika Korps at El Alamein, as well as the allied landings in North Africa. In view of all this, it was likely this soldier's fears of becoming a combat statistic were well founded.

I said, "OK, I'll tell you what I can do. But first, I must talk to some people. The Tatra Mountains are not extensive, so there are not many places where you can get lost, or hide. Do you have something personal or small issued by the army that still could be noticed if left on a trail?" He could offer nothing but an "official issue" handkerchief. "All right, we can use something like that," I told him. "My mind is starting to think of a plan ... maybe a strategy we might use." When the restaurant owner approached our table, I asked him to prepare four more trout for us the next evening at 6:00 P.M. I told my "friend" to be prompt so that we could work out a plan for what I suggested would be our last meeting.

After assuring myself that I was not being followed, I made my way to meet Zosia, my AK contact, at her house in the Zakopane area. I explained, to her initial disbelief, my encounter with the young German officer and his plea for help in escaping the Eastern Front. Finally convinced, she gave me instructions to pass on to the officer about where he could rendezvous with an AK member, whose orders he would have to follow. She told me to arrange for a few drops of blood on the handkerchief, which they would leave on a bush along a decoy route into the mountains. We agreed that it was unlikely the Germans would send a patrol to search for him since most of the mountainous areas were off limits to their troops. Zosia purposely did not tell me their specific plans beyond the rendezvous plan, again under the principle of "what you don't know...."

The soldier and I met the next evening at the appointed time and enjoyed another trout dinner. I asked him directly if he still intended to go through with his desertion, and he answered without hesitation that he did. I then passed on Zosia's instructions, telling him he would meet a woman who would take him under her charge. He was to accept whatever orders she gave, without questions. I also explained to him that I was purposely not privy to what plans they had for him. He accepted this without comment. "So," I said, "since we have little time left, could you please draw a picture again on this tablecloth — this time of a castle?" He smiled, and replied, "With pleasure." So it was that another magnificent drawing went with me on my return to Warsaw. As we said good-bye and shook hands, I again cautioned him: "Look, you have to be aware that the Gestapo operates throughout this area. So, don't talk to anyone, or confide in anyone what you are about to do." I left him at the restaurant and returned the next morning to Warsaw. I have no idea whether he was successful in surviving his desertion and the war. I hoped that he would and one day would call me. In any event, he has remained on my mind forever. I only regret that his name is lost to me, as well as his army division. On a few occasions in later years, when I met certain Germans who might have an interest, I would ask for advice in conducting a search for him. But, in the end, I would start with virtually nothing.

At home, I spread the drawing of the girl on my bed. My mother came and cried out in astonishment at such a beautiful drawing: "I never saw such a beautiful girl in my life! This is absolutely incredible. Who is the artist?"

"Well, he is a German soldier — I call him the 'second Dürer.'" I then explained my meeting with the artist, omitting any mention of his desertion.

Still excited, she told me, "Let's frame both drawings before they are damaged." Then after I told her about the girl, she looked somewhat stern. "How could you keep this woman to yourself. You must bring her home, and introduce her to the family!"

Regrettably, that never occurred, as her untimely death prevented it. The shock of her passing completely erased my memory of her name. My mother and I placed the two drawings in simple frames for safekeeping, but they have not been seen again.

CHAPTER 9

Four Stories, 1943

My Underground Marriage

One late afternoon in the fall of 1943, while I was visiting my uncle Jan at his apartment, we were interrupted by a knock on the door. Opening it, I found myself facing an attractive young woman asking for Jan Rosinski. She was blessed with beautiful blond hair, blue eyes and a demeanor that drew attention. Completely taken aback, I replied, "Elder or the younger?" Looking momentarily puzzled, she answered, "I believe the younger." "Well, that's me," I said, waiting for good fortune to descend on me. I invited her in, but she only stepped into the entry. Thus, I quickly sensed this was no social call. Then the most incredible conversation ensued.

Without introducing herself, she looked forcefully straight into my eyes and said, "I am under orders requiring that you be available to marry me. Please don't ask any questions, because I cannot answer them. You are instructed to come to the Saint Zbawiciel Roman Catholic Church for the ceremony." She specified the date and time, which was only four days away. She also instructed me to meet with the priest two days before the marriage to sign documents and arrange the ceremony. The priest would be expecting me. She again swore me to secrecy. The only explanation she gave for calling on my involvement was that I and my family, presumably my father and mother, lived for a short time in Russia, where I was born, and that she must travel there on an assignment very soon.

Needless to say, I remained stunned, absolutely speechless. Before I could collect my wits, she thanked me for my cooperation — I don't think I had time to offer it — and repeated the time and place for the ceremony. Then she was gone. My uncle could not help hearing some of our conversation, so I asked him for his opinion as to what I should do. He was as puzzled as I, thinking the woman might be a provocation. However, he demurred from telling me what I should do by saying, "Jan, just be careful." We both thought it unusual that the AK command would direct a stranger to me with such a personal request without first alerting me. Yet, this was sometimes the haphazard way decisions were made and carried out. I might have been able to refuse the so-called order without facing disciplinary action.

Nevertheless, on that auspicious day, I dressed in my best suit and presented myself at the church several minutes early and in a very nervous state. She arrived within minutes, and we then proceeded into the church. As we approached the altar, the priest appeared to be pleased to see us, as he greeted us with a welcoming smile. I sensed that he might have been under orders from the AK as well. If so, it was yet another service performed by the Catholic Church for the resistance. When our vows were exchanged, I felt her cold hand, realizing then that she must have been just as nervous as I. That helped to convince myself that she really was a spy and risking her life for Poland. After the priest's blessing, we turned and walked back down the aisle and right past a group of Gestapo and SS officers. One, who appeared to be the senior SS officer, approached us and offered his compliments to the "beautiful bride and handsome groom." He handed me his official card with a crisp formality. Glancing at his name, a cold realization hit me straight on. The officer looking at me, obviously for a reaction, was SS Brigadeführer Jürgen Stroop, the major general who commanded the SS in Warsaw and who oversaw the destruction of the Warsaw ghetto. Complimenting us again, he invited us to their officers club on Aleja Szucha the next night for a dinner party. We thanked him, and then slowly made our way out of the church.

As we exited the church, another obstacle appeared on the path in front of us. Two Gestapo officers were scrutinizing worshippers passing by and picking some out for ID checks. My new bride pulled me aside to tell me to walk her back to her apartment, which was nearby. Once there, she told me to see her into the building and then walk around the building and be on my way. She made it firmly clear that there was to be no more contact. I recall vaguely that she said she was British, or working with the British. My curiosity simply wouldn't let me end our relationship quite yet. After seeing her to the door of the apartment building, I lingered at some distance from behind the building to see if she would emerge and give some clue as to what she was all about. After an hour, I walked slowly toward a small square, where there was a trolley stop.

I was about to walk on when I noticed a poorly dressed woman, perhaps a cleaning lady, approaching the square. She wore an old scarf over her head, but this did not disguise the fact that she was "my wife." She saw me turn toward her, and then made clear motions to warn me away. This was my last sight of this determined and dedicated woman, whose name I failed to remember, if, in fact, I ever knew her true name. After the war, walking through some crowded square in London, I heard a voice weakly calling out "Janek," my nickname. It may have been my imagination, but perhaps not. My thoughts still return occasionally to that wedding day, as well as to the unexpected encounter with General Stroop. We were fortunate that he did not intrude again in our lives. He had other distractions that ultimately would send him to the gallows.

Stroop was arrested by the Soviet NKVD in 1945. While in a Polish prison, Stroop told his tale, with little deception, to a fellow prisoner, Kazimierz Moczarski, a journalist and former AK officer. The resulting book, *Conversations with an Executioner*, is a no-holds-barred account of Stroop's life. With nothing left to lose, Stroop was very open about his misdeeds, and Moczarski, who was knowledgeable about the Polish resistance, did a superb job of turning their two years in a cell into a nonstop interview. The book that resulted gives as good a portrait as one can have of the actual perpetrators of the Holocaust. Stroop was executed after his second trial in 1952 at the site of the Ghetto Uprising (Davies, p. 558).

The Casino

Later in 1943, Adam Orzechowski, one of my closest friends and a classmate in the chemistry department at WIT, came to me and confided that German officials had offered him a job working in a casino they planned to open in the area of Aleje Ujazdowskie. The Germans had seized one of the many palatial homes there for their enterprise. We all needed money, so here was an opportunity for him to earn a decent salary. Adam spoke German and French perfectly, so he would be well qualified. I encouraged him to go ahead and take the job. I would explain to my friends and contacts about our conversation and that he should not be punished in any way for working for the Germans. No one should question his loyalty as he also was a lieutenant in the Polish Army artillery reserve. Adam Orzechowski probably suspected my involvement with the AK, and by asking for my opinion on the job, he would be insuring his safety from any punitive action by the AK. The next day, Adam called me to report that he had been accepted and would start his job in a day or two. This gave me the opportunity I had been looking for. I passed word to my AK conspirators that I now have a man working on the inside of the casino and he will be "our man." I advised the AK command that Adam is a bright fellow, a good chemist, and we can use him for our work. We saw the casino as a place to gather intelligence, and also as a target for sabotage or destruction.

I then called Jozef "Joe" Bulhak, a lieutenant in the regular Polish Army, who was an adventurous swashbuckler of a character, and sometimes too handsome for his own good. Joe came from a noble family, with the financial resources to support his active social life. We often hiked together in the mountains and enjoyed playing tennis, but most of this was before the Germans intruded on us. Without giving a reason, I told Joe to take a pencil and paper and write down for memory the following sentence: "Very small birds are singing beautifully in the spring in Zakopane." "Now, do you have it?" I asked. Joe said he did, so I told him, if this phrase is ever mentioned to you, take a pistol and kill Adam Orzechowski!" "What, how could this be, " he blurted out, "he's your best friend for heaven's sake!" I paused a moment, then replied, "Look, Joe, we don't have friends in war. I truly hope this will never happen, but don't ask questions. This is what I want you to do in case he turns out to be a traitor." Joe reluctantly accepted my request, thus ending the matter for now.

A few days later, walking near my institute, I passed Professor Zawadzki, a specialist in inorganic chemical technology in our department. Apparently knowing of my acquaintance with Adam Orzechowski, Zawadzki stopped me to say, "You know Jan, Adam is working for the Germans at their new casino." I acknowledged what he said, and started to defend Adam, but was abruptly cut off. The professor was in no mood for discussion. "I will do everything to see that he will never graduate. He will be thrown out and never to return when we have a free Poland."

I looked the professor in the eye, knowing that he had lost a son in the AK, and told him, "Adam will graduate from this institute, I guarantee you!"

Glowering at me, he nearly yelled, "No he cannot. It will be impossible!"

"Sir, I guarantee he will graduate!"

Seeing no purpose in continuing this conversation, I walked away. After a few steps, I looked back, and saw that Professor Zawadzki had also looked back at me, with a puzzled look on his face over what had just transpired. The matter was never raised again.

The AK command approved Adam's task as an informant. At the outset, we had no specific instructions for him other than to concentrate on his job and please his "masters." I told him to observe the presence of high ranking German officers and any Poles who might visit there as guests. I had hoped Adam would become a valuable operative for the AK, especially in a place where there is drinking and loose talk. In the end, we decided to blow up the casino, but the actual command kept being postponed. No one wanted to incite the Germans for revenge killings of innocent Poles, so the casino continued operating at least through the rest of the year.

The Virgin

On a Sunday afternoon, I had an unexpected visitor at my apartment, a young woman and student at WIT. After a brief social chat, I asked her the purpose of her visit. After a short pause, she blurted out that she could no longer go on living under the stress of the occupation. Although to my knowledge she was not in the underground, she said she feared arrest and possible death at any time. Cutting her off, I replied, "Look, we all have to survive — we can do nothing else. Someday, this will all be over." She lamented that she had nothing to live for, adding that she was a virgin. "Of course," I quickly interjected. "You come from a respectable family, so I would expect nothing else of you. But why are you telling this to me?" Tears now welling in her eyes, she said, "Well, before I die, I would like to know what it would be like to have a married life … to have sex."

I knew now that I was facing a very troubled woman, and that what I said now might influence whether she chose to live or possibly take her own life. "Please don't do what you are thinking. Don't do this to yourself. You have your whole life ahead of you." Avoiding my eyes, she nearly pleaded: "Then, can I stay with you?" "No," I quickly replied, "I'm sorry, that's not possible." I kept insisting she not pursue her intentions, but she insisted she must. My mother arrived at the apartment at this point and joined in the conversation after I explained the nature of the woman's visit. We both continued to caution her and urged her to survive for a better life to come. Finally, she left, leaving the tension of this bizarre conversation hanging in the room.

About three months later, she came to the apartment again. Perhaps too sternly, I asked her, "Well, what is it this time?" Blushing and in anguish, she confessed that she was pregnant. I could only admonish her for doing something we had counseled her against: "So, what is it that you want me to do?" She said she had access to one kilogram of morphine in the institute's chemistry lab, which could be used as an anesthesia during an abortion. We talked about this further. I told her that the morphine she spoke of had been solidified and destroyed in a bombing and fire. Trying to stall her, I told her I would think all this over. Finally, after mulling it over, I asked Dr. Sikorska at her hospital if she would be willing to perform the abortion. Her first response was, "Is it yours?" "Of course not," I said, but she refused to help.

Two weeks later, I learned through the AK that she had been grabbed by a German patrol and taken in a van to Gestapo headquarters on Aleja Szucha. When they opened the van, she was found dead, having taken a suicide pill. It was not entirely uncommon to carry one if there was an immediate threat to your life, especially if you had secrets to protect. So that was the fate of one distraught student, who found an unfortunate answer to her lack of will to live. Yet, this was not uncommon among the citizens of Warsaw, young or old.

Anna on the Street

At an AK meeting, I was asked by one senior officer about my chemistry experience outside the WIT chemistry department. The objective he had in mind was to acquire infectious chemical substances and spread them on German trains returning westward from the Eastern Front, many of them carrying wounded troops. My immediate reaction was one of hesitancy in mounting an operation that would kill wounded soldiers, who could not defend themselves. Targeting regular, active troops was okay. We ended up in a heated argument on the right and wrong of such a tactic. However, in the end, I held my ground and the commander did not press me on the matter. But he went away highly angered at my obstinacy. Then one week later, my attitude suddenly changed, which I conveyed to the commander. What abruptly changed my mind was the news that my good friend Wlodek Krynicki was killed in another operation against the Germans. This greatly upset me and set me on a new course of action.

While all this was circulating in my mind, I was walking one afternoon along Aleje Jerozolimskie when I saw a German patrol on the street stopping and questioning Polish women. Suddenly, a young woman walked up to my side and slipped her arm under mine, in what could only be described as a very friendly gesture. While I was gathering my wits, she tilted her head towards mine and said, "My name is Anna, and I would like you to be my husband for this moment." Having just noted the patrol, it was clear what her intentions were. Smiling, she added, "They may just be looking for prostitutes, but could you help me through that line of police?" So, what could I say but Okay: "Well, I'm Jan, and it's nice to meet my wife Anna." We were not stopped, so thanking me, she replied, "Let's just keep walking together a little farther away from these men."

Finally, I had a chance to look at her. She was really quite attractive. When we arrived at her apartment building, I nearly pleaded: "You really don't have to thank me, I would just like to talk to you." "Well, you can," she said. "It seems you refused to help in a plan to attack German trains carrying wounded soldiers, but that now you have reconsidered." Now in a state of shock, I could only muster a "what!" Undeterred, she plowed right ahead. "The plans have been changed and someone else is now in command of the operation."

"Well, that's fine," I said. "Since Krynicki was killed, I'd like to seek my own revenge."

"All right then. You will be given an envelope of powder. A man in a German army uniform will deliver it to your apartment, and he will also instruct you in how to handle it. We really need your help in this."

"Okay, that's fine, except a big problem — if my mother sees what she thinks is a German soldier in her apartment. She does not know about my work with the AK and I don't want to have to explain this business to her." Finally, I realized it was a possible problem I would have to deal with when it arose.

Anna smiled with relief: "Thank you for getting back in this business." We then embraced and kissed.

Before she could move an inch, I asked, "When and where can I meet you again?"

"No, it's over now. This is our last meeting. You must forget about me. I did my part, now it's time for you to do yours."

It was about a week before the first package arrived and was left at my door. Better not to open it here, I decided, so I took it to a nearby park and gently opened it downwind. It was really a powder substance, something like flour in appearance. I took my pocketknife and probed some lumps. *What do I do now?* I asked myself. I figured I would just drop small amounts of the powder on the floors of the passenger train cars and let shoes and the air do the rest. I went back to the apartment to await instructions that Anna had promised. Finally, the "German soldier" arrived later in the afternoon and instructed me in handling the substance, which he said might be pneumonia bacteria. He also remarked that he believed it had been supplied by the British, but he offered no further explanation.

He spoke Polish but was not a Pole. He departed and I was now left to my own devices. It was suggested that I acquire a German army uniform, or that one would be provided. However, there was a high risk in such a disguise. An army uniform would have to come with orders or ID and I had none. If I was questioned while on the train, that would be it! Finally, I settled on a Hitler Youth (*Hitler Jugend*) uniform. With the uniform, I was able to board a multiuse troop train at the main city station that was heading to an unknown destination westward toward Germany. I should give credit here to the AK and their capability of acquiring German uniforms, equipment and some small arms weapons from quartermaster stores of the German army. These, for the most part, were cash transactions that even included ancient Roman gold coins. Gold was the preferred currency. I also used identity papers I forged myself indicating I was a *Volksdeutsche*— a foreign-born ethnic German. This was not an easy task, as I had to research every detail and have it checked more than once by a trusted source in the underground. Fortunately, my spoken German, although not perfect, was good enough to match the documentation. In any event, my disguise worked well enough that I wasn't thrown off the train. On more than a few occasions, wearing normal clothes, I was ordered off the train — actually thrown off— by Polish conductors, who had no appreciation for my German documentation. It is likely that some of these railway workers were AK members.

After sitting a while in a third-class car, I started my walk through several cars, while dropping small amounts of the powder on the floors as I went. One moment I thought I might have drawn the attention of some soldiers standing and talking in the aisle, but I passed without arousing their suspicion. My nerves were on edge, however, and I found a temporary hiding place in a toilet. I was able to exit the train at the next stop not far from the station of departure. I had a change of clothes in a satchel bag so that I would not draw attention to myself once off the train. I never learned the results of this operation, but I believe it was a success.

Another week passed, and a second envelope arrived at my apartment, and the soldier contact followed. This was a different powder, something like crystal particles, but my contact could not explain what it was. I had published a number of chemistry papers on fine particles, but I had no microscope or other lab equipment to analyze it. So, I decided to take the precaution of getting an antiviral shot. This was a most unpleasant experience, as the injection was in my stomach. I was still nervous about any contact with this substance, so I ended up spreading it in only one railcar before exiting the train. I rode the trains about 25 kilometers from Warsaw before getting off at the Otwock station. I then made my way back home through secondary roads, still wearing the Hitler Youth uniform. Fortunately, except for one incident, I was not recognized before reaching the safety of my apartment. I was spotted by a girl in the building, and she reacted to my uniform in a state of shock. Cutting her short, I simply told her to "shut up and don't ask questions!" I think she instinctively knew what I was about. She likely was in the AK herself. I never received a report or any information on the results of this activity, but I believe it too was successful.

I also used this powder at least four times in two hospitals in Warsaw taken over by the German army. My friend Dr. Sikorska was chief surgeon at three hospitals in the city, so if I was questioned by Germans, I used her name as the person I was visiting. Because of the shortage of German doctors, she was constantly on call for surgery on German patients. I also had my occupational and *Volksdeutsche* papers with me. I did alert her that the AK was targeting the hospitals, but omitted that I was the one doing it. She protected herself by taking the necessary antidotes. It was apparent the chemicals were having an effect, as Dr. Sikorska told me many German soldiers had become sick. I felt no remorse. If they were released from the hospital for duty they would be killing Poles again.

To my knowledge, I believe I may have been the only person in the AK in Warsaw who carried out these so-called chemical attacks. Apparently, the one exception was the son of Professor Zawadzki of WIT's chemistry department. I do not recall his first name but, regrettably, he was killed in this same type of operation. When I learned of this, I called on the professor to extend my condolences. However, when we met, it was too emotional for either of us. We exchanged silent handshakes and parted.

There was one other fellow who proved quite inventive and courageous whom I learned about years later. Jan, who came from the province of Poznan and spoke German fluently, raised and traded in pigs before the war. During and after the war, the region from which he came endured the most atrocious sufferings under the domination of the Germans. Coming to Warsaw, Jan became one of the many specialists in paying back the Germans with their own coin. To spread contagious diseases was Jan's favorite activity. He carried on his person an astounding collection of every type of lethal agent. He had an attractive, specially constructed little box in which he housed lice that bore microbes, typhoid-bearing germs and others.

He would frequent bars, enter into conversation with German soldiers, and drink with them. Drinking was one of Jan's pleasures, but he never let it interfere with his main objective. At the proper moment he would drop louse-bearing typhoid germs behind the collar of his German friend. He would also drop germs into their drinks and introduce them to girls who had venereal diseases. Jan was known to have a number of different methods he would utilize according to his convenience or fancy. Not one of the Germans with whom the "walking germ," as he was known, became acquainted ever escaped lightly (Karski, p. 258).

CHAPTER 10

Warsaw Uprising

Among historians and, especially, the Poles who experienced them, the events that exploded on the streets of Warsaw on the afternoon of August 1, 1944, remain in controversy — both for how they were conceived, and then how they were carried out. Thousands of men, women and children inside and outside the organized resistance who perhaps could have survived the war and occupation ended up in makeshift graves. I know because I buried brave souls on that first day of fighting. Perhaps in the psychic of the Polish people it was inevitable. The solidarity of the city's citizens was surely unparalleled in modern history and was not repeated until the famous Solidarity movement rose up against communist tyranny nearly four decades later.

Ironically, my occasional exchanges with Russian officers stationed in Warsaw as part of Russian intelligence there revealed their astonishment as to why I was so much against Soviet Russia. To them Poland had been abandoned by the USA and would be incorporated into Soviet Russia and this was to be our future. On one hand I would believe them that Poland had been abandoned, if not sold out, but on the other I nourished a shadow of hope that this might not be true and the only reason they would say such things was because of their expectation that our Underground Army would begin to cooperate with Russia. Nonetheless, I had a terrifying premonition that the first version might be the true one. Three months before the outbreak of the Warsaw Uprising we held a meeting in one of Warsaw's districts, called Zoliborz, where we discussed the possibilities of the uprising. One of those present, a young lieutenant, was explaining to us that the uprising would be necessary because when the Russians would enter the city they would find Warsaw already in the hands of the Polish government.

For my part, personally, I was against the uprising. I reacted strongly, explaining that even should the Germans retreat and should we repossess and occupy Warsaw (actually the only possibility of our achieving this would be a result of German capitulation), then the Russians, upon entering, would simply align against a wall all the members of the entire government and get them shot. This would be "The Grand Finale" of the Polish government.

I further explained to the young lieutenant that Poland's greatest enemy was Soviet Russia. I emphasized at the same time that the information in my possession, obtained through my intelligence work, indicated that we had been sold out by the USA and Great Britain into the hands of Soviet Russia — to my mind greatest enemy Poland ever had, has now, or will have. This was my considered personal opinion. I was trying also to convince my immediate superiors and commanders that Poland, especially at this particular moment, found herself in a very difficult and painful situation, to which there was simply no solution. She found herself, so to speak, between "the hammer and anvil" because on one hand we faced the Germans and on the other Soviet Russia, which was the menace. Thus, our AK situation was extremely difficult and, in principle, impossible to bring a solution to. To me, the only practical solution would be to wait for the Russian spring offensive, which would, hopefully, drive the Germans out of Warsaw.

As stated above, this was my own point of view and, sadly, I had the feeling that nobody was really interested in it. It was clear to me that, as regards the uprising, different decisions were being made and no one would take into consideration my opinions and that my efforts to at least postpone it were fruitless — that whatever we would decide and do would turn, unfortunately, to tragedy. It was clear to me that the 250,000 men and women, instead of continuing to live and work for their homeland would instead uselessly die, without adequate supplies of arms, ammunition, food, water, medication, and receiving no help from the Russians or Western Allies, fighting an enemy who, by contrast, had all of this.

Two weeks before the uprising was launched, two AK commanders, a man and a woman, came to my apartment to request that I take on a new assignment. I was asked to assume charge of a special military security unit tasked with tracking down infiltrators, snipers and anyone who attempted to penetrate the AK's operations. My first response was a question: "Are you collecting the worst SOBs you can find for this duty?" After discussing the matter a few minutes longer, I accepted what really was an order. I was told to await further instructions. Two or three days later, I was contacted again by the man, but again was instructed to stand by. I asked about the woman, who had first accompanied him. After some hesitation, he told me she had been killed while performing courier duty. In the end, no one returned to give me further orders, so I missed my first opportunity at command. My rank as an officer candidate and platoon leader (podchorazy) was not lofty. However, I must confess I made up for my modest status with a rather brazen attitude toward the events that were about to unfold in Warsaw.

Three days before the uprising, I was summoned to an AK meeting called by AK commanders in the city. I and the others assembled there were told that the uprising would achieve great things. Our success, they said, would enable us to join with the allies to defeat the Germans, who were now fighting on two fronts. As the briefer, a young lieutenant continued to voice his optimistic predictions, and I could no longer hold my growing frustration: "The Germans will simply destroy us! The Hermann Goering Division is poised on the outskirts of the city. They will burn Warsaw to the ground! We will not meet up with any allies or the Russian army because we will not exist." There was stony silence in the room. (In fact, elements of the division's regiments were ordered into the fighting during the uprising, primarily in the Wola district, on the western side of the city center, where many civilian executions took place. After taking part in the crushing of the resistance, the division was later recalled to the defense of Germany.) The officer turned to me and finally could only say, "Well, we must fight the best we can." "Fight with what?" I asked. He replied, "We just need to launch the uprising."

"I'm for action, but not suicide," I almost shouted back. "We need to survive this occupation to be the new leadership for Poland after the war, after Germany is defeated. We can't do that from the grave. This is nothing but suicide. Are those orders for people without arms?" I spoke without regard to rank or status, and I was the only one present to do so. No one else voiced any objections. Finally in exasperation, I blurted out, "Did you all lose your minds?"

As events turned out, that was my last meeting with my AK commanders. Nominally, I served in a group in the City Center District, or region, that included the areas of Marszalkowska, Piekna and Nowy Swiat streets. The region was commanded by a Colonel "Radwan," whom I rarely, if ever, saw during the uprising. One of my self-appointed duties at that time was as a chemical expert responsible for transport of chemical weapons from a hidden depot at Krucza Street No. 9 to different AK units, and chemicals for medical use to military hospitals at Mokotowska Street No.

55 and Hoza Street No. 13. Means of transport, when security allowed, was by handcart or horse-drawn cart. Most of the nonmedical chemicals were not lethal, but could cause sickness and vomiting and conceivably put German troops out of commission for days or weeks. I did turn up from World War I stocks one cylinder of a poisonous fosgene gas that attacked the lungs and two cylinders of nerve gas. Both of these outdated chemicals might prove to be unstable if released, so I avoided using them.

An alert was sent out to all AK elements by runners the afternoon of July 31, ordering the uprising to be launched at the "W-hour" of 5:00 P.M., August 1, 1944. Perhaps I was no longer regarded as important, as I learned of the order indirectly by word of mouth.

On August 1, 1944, at about 3.00 P.M. I was walking to see my close friend Stefan Kawecki on Krucza Street when I suddenly heard the first gunshots. "My God!" I exclaimed to myself, "it's started already!" Suddenly, a squad of AK soldiers were running toward me, yelling, "We have German prisoners." They were pushing along with them five or six prisoners, who, as they came closer, looked about as young and scared as us. They were from the elite Hermann Goering Division and willingly gave up more information than name, rank and serial number. For whatever reason, I took pity on one German. I dug into my pocket for a wrapped piece of bread and cut off some with my knife and handed it to this shaking member of the "Master Race." He looked too shaken to speak, but nodded his head in acknowledgment of my momentary generosity. Since I wore the cap of the Warsaw Institute of Technology, they evidently decided that I would be trustworthy and asked me what they should do with the German prisoners. "I really don't know what you should do," I replied, explaining further that they had their own commanders whom they should ask about it and that to my mind it would be nonsense to keep them prisoners in a situation in which we ourselves were short on food and supplies. This simply would not be practical, while to mistreat them in any way would go against the Geneva Convention.

We then came under heavy fire coming from Krucza Street, and I dove for the protection of a nearby wall. Two members of the AK squad who were acquaintances appeared to be mortally wounded. I myself had taken fragments of a bullet and stone wall in my hand and arm, but it was not serious. As the firing lessened, I tried to carry the two downed AK soldiers to the safety of a courtyard, but I was too weak to carry them. Finally, I was able to drag each one inside the gate of an apartment building courtyard. Both men had died before medical help could be called. I could see no place to bury them. I called out to a resident of the building for help.

He gave me a shovel and allowed me to dig a grave in the only place where there was sufficient soil, and that was the flower beds along the inside of the courtyard wall.

Next, I continued on my way to the Kawecki apartment. On reaching his place, Stefan pulled his concealed radio out of the heating stove, where he had kept it in secrecy throughout the German occupation, and let me know that just now he had received the news of the start of the Uprising from the Polish radio station in London.

"I know it already since I just heard the first gun shots and I met several young men members AK who captured several German prisoners," I replied. "This is the end, since there is no way we could survive this hell." As I had mentioned earlier, I had been against the uprising, or at least suggested its postponement, but what could I do! Nothing.

I also informed Kawecki that about one week before the uprising began someone from the AK came to see me and asked would I agree to be transferred from the Intelligence Investigative Branch to the Military Corps of Security Service (Korpus Sluzby Bezpieczenstwa). I stated that if this was an order, then I would expect to receive specific instructions as to what I was to do along with new commanders. I was informed that everything would be made clear in a few days. I agreed to all of this and was accordingly transferred. I told Kawecki that I was awaiting new assignments. After that I decided to return to our apartment on Marszalkowska Street 95 where I stayed with my mother. The building itself was of importance since it had in its yard an independent water pump from which anyone could draw clear and clean drinking water. Mother was not at home, so I left her a brief note on the table informing her that I was returning to my friend Stefan's apartment, or I might stop on my way at Smolna Street, thinking that my mother could have gone to the Branickis' residence where I would meet her.

Back on the street trying to cross Nowogrodzka Street, already then I stumbled on many corpses lying on the ground, especially where Nowogrodzka and Poznanska streets crossed and where a solidly built big building housing the post office stood. The Germans occupied this building and used its roof as an excellent observation point and a place to shoot from. In view of this, Nowogrodzka Street was impassable. I concluded that first I would go to Smolna Street, and I ran across onto the other side of Marszalkowska Street, where the bullets were hitting the ground all around me. Nonetheless I continued down Marszalkowska up to Aleje Jerozolimskie then right towards the Vistula River and towards Smolna Street to find my mother.

My attention was drawn again to the post office building, as the German gun crews on the roof had sweeping fields of fire over three streets. Next to me was a young man walking who had just been shot. Suddenly he fell to the ground screaming with incredible pain. At the same time a middle-aged man ran up to him and began to drag him as I joined him to help. We were able to move him to the staircase of the closest building in Aleje Jerozolimskie. We put the wounded young man on the stairway, head up, and this is when the middle-aged man who was helping the victim hurriedly told me, "I must act quickly to remove the bullets from him, because first, he is bleeding heavily and secondly both his legs are shot. I am Doctor Bentkowski and colonel in the Polish Army. Can you help me?" I was surprised as he was well known in the capital. "Of course I'll help you. What can I do?"

"First, bring a large bottle or bucket of water, and get some bandages. Just go to one of the apartments in this building and take bedsheets and tear them into strips." He then pulled a knife from his pocket. "This is all I have, but one thing is certain, it is very sharp." "OK, I'll go for water and I'll be right back." I knocked on the door of the closest apartment, and a young woman opened the door. She was scared at first since I was stained with the blood of the wounded young man, but she gave me a pair of scissors and a bucket of clean water and some sheets that I tore into bandage strips.

When I returned, Dr. Bentkowski was ready to go to work. "He is semiconscious, so why don't you sit on him so he won't move. I'm going to have to cut him open."

I suggested that I should rather lie flat on him since that way my weight would be evenly distributed over his body, making it impossible for him to move. We cut his pants open, and we took off his shoes. Luckily, one bullet had passed through his thigh without damaging the bone and a second bullet was imbedded deeply in his lower leg. This second one probably ricocheted from the sidewalk or from the street and hit his leg with lesser impact, causing smaller damage.

The doctor looked momentarily hesitant. Looking closely at the leg wound, I suggested to him, "Why don't you try and extract the bullet, not from the entrance wound, but from the other side as it might offer easier access." Taken aback, he replied, "What are you, a doctor?" "No, I'm a chemist, and chemical engineer. I'm sorry, it's just a suggestion." "Actually, that's a good idea," he said as he felt for the bullet.

The man could understand what we were saying. I acknowledged that he was in great pain, but I needed to sit on him so he couldn't move while the doctor worked on him. I tried to talk to him but he almost immediately became unconscious. Doctor Bentkowski removed the bullet from his leg and successfully controlled the bleeding. He did so expertly, cleaned both wounds and wrapped them in the torn sheets. We moved him from the staircase, as carefully as possible, to the closest apartment, the one belonging to the young woman who had helped us earlier. We asked her to provide him with a shelter, and laid him, all three of us, on a bed. There was no food available, but I could not wait any longer and left. The residents would have to take care of him now. Such, then, was my first day of my encounter with the Warsaw Uprising.

Next Dr. Bentkowski said, "I have to rush to the hospital now." However, I suggested that first we should perhaps check what was going on in the Aleje Jerozolimskie area where the firing was constant and dead people were lying all over the place. Those who were not successful in fleeing were simply killed. Otherwise, in view of this, I asked whether we should perhaps just wait in this building until dark to move more safely to our respective destinations. This we eventually did. As we discussed, Dr. Bentkowski mentioned that he could not give me any direct orders since he was not my direct commander but he asked me at the same time whether I could not be of help to various hospitals in providing various medical supplies for the wounded patients, of whom there would be many. He further pointed out that the hospitals were not adequately prepared or equipped for such an emergency and would consequently require all the help possible from outside sources.

To this I replied that should the doctor indicate any place, warehouse or address, I would be happy to do so. He did give me some addresses on a street parallel to Marszalkowska Street which I remembered well because of a kefir store, "Kasinski," where, before the war, I occasionally would stop to buy some fresh kefir.

At dusk, after saying a brief good-bye to each other, we parted. Dr. Bentkowski went to his hospital while I went toward Marszalkowska Street, where the firing had stopped and which at this time was relatively safe. I wanted to continue towards Nowogrodzka Street but could not reach it because at that point the firing was intense there, especially from the machine guns. Consequently, I decided to turn back to Marszalkowska Street, moving close to the wall to reach our apartment to find out whether my mother was at home. I walked into our apartment on the fourth floor; my note still was lying on the table but my mother was not in.

I decided to return to Stefan Kawecki's place for the night. On seeing him, and admittedly in a state of heightened anxiety, I said, "Now it begins, they will kill us all!" Stefan gave me a troubled look, and then told me he heard that the Russians were moving closer to the Vistula River and the eastern outskirts of the city. "So, help may be coming," he said. I laughed. "That won't happen. The Russians won't help us at all."

We were too exhausted and worried to argue. In the morning, together with Stefan, I went to the second floor to check out, through one of the windows, what the situation on Krucza Street was like. Suddenly, as we peered through the window, a big bomb hit the street with a thundering blast and we saw distinctly something which broke away from the bomb itself and rolled towards the wall of a nearby building, filling the air with a smell of some gas, which I thought was presumably benzene. It was obviously an incendiary bomb. Miraculously the fuse did not ignite. After all this, I jokingly remarked to Stefan that if we survived this incident then we would surely survive the entire Warsaw Uprising. We looked through the window again and we saw a small German tank moving from Marszalkowska Street through to Krucza Street towards the Vistula River.

We ran out of the building towards the main building gate and when the tank approached I pulled out of my pocket the only grenade I had and threw it at the tank. It bounced off the side of the turret and exploded on the other side of the street, in front of a barber shop, shattering a window and door. The result was that we demolished a barber shop. I said to Stefan, "This is my contribution to the uprising — I blew up a barber shop!" The tank, meanwhile, quickly backed up to Marszalkowska Street and headed towards the Saski Garden. This was my first close encounter with the Germans, and I lost my only grenade. Stefan and I had stopped and were sitting away from the street in a courtyard. We found a vacated apartment and I suggested we stay there for a while. We had an open view of the street below and soon spotted an artillery or tank shell that had landed in the street. It had not exploded, but broke apart, revealing a strange canister. We moved down to the street to examine it, but decided to leave it as it lay. It looked like it might be poison gas.

Worried, I briefly left Stefan and went back again to our apartment but my mother was not there and so I left her a second note telling her that I was still alive and safe. Going back to rejoin Stefan, while on my way I decided to check also on my aunt Zofia Gedroyc's house on Hoza Street. I found out that everyone was O.K. and so I continued back to Stefan. I decided to sleep there, rather than risk capture or worse on the streets. There was little food to eat, but Stefan thought our survival warranted a small celebration, so he insisted we have a drink of vodka. I tossed the drink down and that's the last I remember until the next morning. At daybreak, I told him that I intended to join our forces and fight the Germans. I had taken an armband with the red and white Polish national colors from a fallen soldier, so all I needed now was a weapon. I eventually found a revolver, which essentially was useless, and then I managed to steal someone's shotgun and shells, also not much use against a trained enemy. I shot at one sniper on a rooftop, to little effect. I had received no direct orders or instructions from the AK command as to a unit assignment, so I came to the conclusion that I would fight the war my own way.

Subsequently, I resolved, together with Stefan, to build a barricade on Marszalkowska Street. It took us two days of nonstop work to finish it. Yet, immediately thereafter a German tank went through it easily, destroying it all in the process. Thus we learned what kind of material barricades are to be constructed from to be effective, namely concrete blocks positioned vertically.

We were then informed that we were to assist with the construction of a barricade at Aleje Ujazdowskie. I asked why exactly at that place and was told that if it was constructed at that point it would enable us to bypass the Germans, to get behind their positions and to attack their tanks from the rear. While on our way to help with the construction of this barricade I noticed two men who entered the Aleje Ujazdowskie and were immediately shot down. With the help of some young people passing by we dragged the bodies to the back of the building. One of the helpers asked me whether they could take their wallets to inform their families of what happened, to which I replied, "Yes, given the time and opportunity." The bodies were placed by us behind the building, which I believed was some sort of a small printing house of books or newspapers because of big bales of paper we found there. When the Germans opened fire from their tanks and attacked this building, which was falling apart, the bales of paper would not burn in flames but only smolder.

Together with Stefan, we subsequently spent about four days there trying to dig our way through from the cellars of the building, under Ujazdowskie Aleje, to the other side. Unfortunately nothing came out of it. We were only able to put up, vertically, some of the concrete plates removed from the sidewalks, in order to crawl to the other side of the very wide street. Ultimately this entire project remained unfinished. Very simply we were lacking the basic tools such as shovels, crowbars, picks, and we had only one wheel barrow to move the dug out dirt. One more additional, very important and difficult factor which complicated our work was that we were running into many underground pipes of various sizes which made our digging almost impossible.

Not knowing it at the time, this was the last I would see or hear of Stefan for more than six decades. Years later, as I was recollecting these first days of the uprising, I decided to find out what had happened to my good friend. I called my cousin's wife, Maria Giedroyc, in Warsaw and asked her if she could try to find Stefan, that is if he was still alive. She replied that this would pose no problem. Luckily enough she found him in the phone book and called back with his telephone number. I made the call just before Thanksgiving Day 2007. When he answered, I said, "Stefan, this is Jan Rosinski, how are you, old friend?" My greeting was met with silence. Finally, "My God, where are you?" I replied, "I am in the United States, in a city — Boulder, Colorado." I could sense he was in a state of shock. I explained why I had come to contact him and my efforts to record my experiences in the underground. He told me he would like to do the same and mail it to me. Unfortunately, he never managed to do this. However, the very next year, in 2008, during my last trip to Poland, we met for the first time after almost sixty-five years. This was a very special and emotional get-together for both of us, as anyone can well imagine.

Back on the street, as I walked cautiously along Marszalkowska Street, I spotted an approaching German tank formation. The lead tank fired a round from its main gun into a building and then stopped. Strangely, the tank went into reverse at high speed, so the threat was gone for the moment. Approaching the square where the fighting had begun, I spotted my friend Jozef "Joe" Bulhak, the army lieutenant. He asked, "What are you going to do?"

"I'm joining the fighting. That's what the AK forced me to do. That's what those commanders in London did to us. I don't understand why they ordered the uprising. This is totally ridiculous."

"Well, I won't permit you to go to the front lines," Joe replied. "You are maybe the best chemist in all of Poland and we will need you after the war. You need to survive. So why don't you go back to the center of the city where you live and don't do anything stupid."

"I can't. I left a wounded man in an apartment, so I should check on him and, if necessary, help him get to a hospital." We parted then, and wished each other good luck.

When I reached the nearby Maltanski Hospital, a senior doctor on staff told me I could be of great help in finding bandages and other items urgently needed, as their supplies had dwindled to nothing. He told me of a medical storage facility for the Polish army and suggested I ask the commanding officer for assistance. I readily agreed to help, but asked for some men to help carry the supplies. The doctor managed to round up four men for the job. I asked if anyone had been in the regular army. One of them was a corporal whom I designated as second in command should anything happen to me. "Okay then, so let's start marching!" I said. On our way to the warehouse I stopped at my apartment and picked up backpacks I used in my mountain escapades.

Next, we encountered heavy firing along the way but managed to dodge from point to point until we reached the supply depot. A man in uniform came to the entrance and identified himself as the colonel in charge. I explained the situation at the hospital and asked for whatever supplies they could provide, especially bandages. He refused, claiming they must save everything for when the front moved further into the center of the city.

"Well sir, people are dying over there now, so I need you to give us whatever stores are available." He again refused, so I hit him square on the jaw. Stunned, he collapsed on the floor. He yelled at me that I would be court-martialed and hanged for this assault. "Look colonel, I don't care if I'll be hanged or not — by you, Russians, or Germans. Nobody is going to get out of this alive anyway." I then ordered the men to pack up what they could find in the rucksacks we carried and then we would head back to the hospital. The colonel was still dazed as I told him, "I'm taking this piece of paper and writing my name and address on it. So, if you want to court-martial me, you will know where to find me. You do what you want, but I'm just doing my duty as ordered. I'm supposed to deliver bandages, so I'll deliver bandages, and you will not stop me!" He again threatened me as "my corporal" rushed up to me, wide-eyed. "But sir, he's a colonel!" I said, "I don't give a damn. The hospital needs supplies and that's it."

So that's how I continued my service during the uprising. To the surprise of the doctors, we returned to the hospital with a considerable amount of medical supplies. I related to them the entire incident with the colonel. One of the doctors explained to me that that this very colonel was the main commander of all the AK hospitals and that I could run into serious trouble. For my part I felt that I had done everything I should have done and what was my duty. The doctor embraced me and thanked us all. He then wrote out a short letter of appreciation for me, which I folded and put in my pocket. During those days I collected three such letters, all since lost.

With this mission accomplished, my attention was then diverted to finding some way to avoid the deadly firing from German gun positions on the buildings' roofs. Several streets and intersections were subjected to crossing fields of machine-gun fire, as well as from tanks patrolling the streets and often just parked in a fixed firing position. I concluded on my own that we needed to attempt a tunneling operation that would allow passage under Aleje Jerozolimskie, a key four-lane thoroughfare that cut through a strategic section of the city. After observing German vehicle and personnel movements and investigating tunnel entrance and exit routes, I picked an apartment building facing Aleje Jerozolimskie, and a tunnel route that would come out behind the facing building across the street in a park. The park was heavily shaded with trees and bushes that would afford some protection in moving in and out of the tunnel.

I was able to recruit ten men who had been loitering at the Maltanski Hospital but who were not patients. They probably would have preferred to be patients after enduring the next two weeks underground. After briefing AK commanders on my project, they provided some additional recruits, but these proved less than energetic. Some of them just quit after the first few days. We managed to round up basic tools, shovels and picks and wheelbarrows. Finding food for the workers would be a problem, but men sent out at night to forage from houses and apartments were usually met with some sympathy and help. Usually it wasn't much, bread, mostly stale, and cooked potatoes with some vegetables. Meat was almost non-existent. All movement in and out of the building remained risky throughout the operation. Before we even got started, two Polish soldiers were shot in the street in front of the building, but there was nothing we could do to help without endangering us all, and I told the men this. It did not sit well, but I was not challenged.

We started the tunneling in the basement. Dirt was loaded onto canvas sheets and pulled out to the opening, loaded onto wheelbarrows and then dumped in a back alley. The problem of dirt disposal kept the height and width of the tunnel to hands-and-knees crawling. Light and ventilation became a problem that could be only partially alleviated by drilling small holes up to the surface. We had one or two flashlights, but they had to be used sparingly. The biggest obstacles soon proved to be avoiding water mains, sewer pipes, and gas lines. This forced us to take a circuitous route sometimes and resulted in more delays. Added to this was the frequent firing by the Germans above us on the street. Most fearful was the rumble of tanks that loosened dirt overhead. Fortunately we were deep enough so that our "roof" held. We slept in the basement at night, too exhausted to talk. The stench from our labors was nearly overpowering, but there was little we could do to clean or bathe ourselves until we were finished. At least we had a single toilet to use. Two weeks and more than 200 feet later we finally dug out to the park. Fortunately, the exit hole was next to some bushes that helped shield it from view.

I was the first to crawl the distance and exit the tunnel after dark. In dodging a tank stationed on one side of the park, I believe I must have set a new Olympic record for the 100-meter sprint as I dashed from tree to tree. Others followed, while some men left from the building where we had started. I reported the completion of the tunnel to the AK and, as far as I knew, they used it until the end of the uprising on October 2, 1944. Someone in the AK suggested that I organize another tunneling operation, but that was enough for me. We all were fortunate in not being discovered and put before a German firing squad. Had the uprising lasted longer than two months, it might have been worth it to tunnel again. A new assignment, however, came my way.

I returned to the Maltanski Hospital to again offer my services. As I came to the entrance, I met unexpectedly Wanda Fejgin, my Jewish classmate at WIT. I had not seen her since she had twice seen me on the street in company with German officers. Her worst fears surfaced, of course, thinking I had sold my soul to the enemy. She had fled on both occasions and I was unable to find her. I could not stand for this lovely girl to suspect me of being a quisling and a spy. So, I hurriedly tried to explain the circumstances of my being with German officers. I could see she was not yet convinced by my explanation. Before we parted, she told me she was helping the staff of a makeshift hospital that had been converted from a residential building. So I left her with at least some of her suspicions about me intact. Later, I attempted to search for her, but time ran out for both of us. To this day, I am torn by what false impressions she may have had of me. I hope she survived and has had a bountiful life.

At the hospital, the doctor in charge again approached me for help. Their medical supplies had again dwindled to nearly nothing. He told me that, according to the information they had, on the corner of Aleje Jerozolimskie and Aleje Ujazdowskie there was a building occupied by the Germans which they had made as their medical supplies depot for their wounded. I was asked if I could perhaps break into this building and steal some of the supplies available. The same doctor also described the two entrances of the building — the main one from the Aleje Jerozolimskie and the additional one from Aleje Ujazdowskie. The main entrance could not be used because of the German patrols keeping permanent watch there.

After a brief consideration I decided to attempt it, and then mustered seven men, including the former corporal. Each man again took a rucksack and we took strips of bedsheets to wrap glass containers and vials. I also decided that first we must go there and check out very carefully the existing situation. Only then could we get in and take out whatever possible. First I stopped again at my apartment and changed into clean clothes. Being very hungry, I put a few pieces of dry bread into my pocket and made myself some tea from dry apple peels and dry raspberries. Such tea, under the circumstances, turned out very tasty. I also ate a piece of gingerbread which my mother had baked and put the remainder into a metal box and hid it in the kitchen cabinet for the next time. I left the apartment and went back to Aleje Jerozolimskie, where I joined the other AK members.

Moving forward, on reaching Nowogrodzka Street we realized that there was no way to proceed further. From a neighboring building we saw many German tanks on the right side of Lazienki Park. Passing through was therefore impossible, especially in daytime. We retreated and decided that in daytime we would have to move again close enough to Aleje Ujazdowskie and at night we would crawl across to the other side of the Aleje. I issued an order to remove from our arms the white-red bands (our AK identification) in order to avoid the visibility of the white color. We took our backpacks and went ahead. We ran very fast from building to building to Nowogrodzka Street, where luckily nobody shot at us and we found ourselves in a back yard. Between the houses we also spotted the body of a young lady, her head missing, the body totally naked, her dress blown completely off by a grenade blast. We entered an empty and open second floor apartment in a nearby building from which we took some bedsheets and in which we wrapped the body of the young woman. I told the corporal and the others to bury the body as best they could. The corporal, first hesitating, brought the head to place it with the body, and then fainted. "I'm sorry," he said, stirring to consciousness, "I just couldn't look at this beautiful face." We finished digging a shallow grave and buried the nameless woman. As before, I took my pocketknife to cut two small branches and made a cross. We said a short prayer over her body and moved on. We used the tunnel safely and made our way to the nearby depot.

Approaching it, we were confronted with a major problem: three heavy tanks were parked directly in front of the building. Fortunately, we spotted a back door to the depot that appeared to be open. Under cover of darkness, we crawled along a wall to the door, which was unlocked. Moving inside, we took off our shoes to avoid making any noise and started a search in the darkened building. We finally found a storeroom on an upper floor that had what we were looking for. We packed our rucksacks and made ready to exit. The tank crews and guards were still moving about in front of the building, so we decided to rest for a few hours before exiting the depot. During the night, we heard soldiers talking and smoking outside and the occasional sound of a toilet on the first floor.

Finally, we were able to leave without incident and return to the hospital with our contraband. As we unpacked our rucksacks, the doctor exclaimed, "Oh no, these are veterinary medicines, medicines for cats, dogs, horses, etc., but not for people!" It became clear therefore that the building we entered contained medications for animals. Once he saw everything we had taken, he decided that some drugs could be of use, such as vitamins, aspirin and sulfur. He hesitated when he asked if we could make a second try, but I agreed to go back to the depot. We made the second effort successfully, but not without a potentially fatal mishap. It took us longer to locate the needed supplies and we had overslept during the night until daybreak. This made us on our return prey for German patrols. We had no choice but to stay inside the building and then leave late the next night. Fortune was again with us, as the building was only for storage and not occupied by German soldiers. We had carried no food with us, so we were famished by the time we made our way back to the hospital on the second night. Nor could we flush or otherwise use a toilet in the depot for fear of being detected, so a bucket had to do. Not wanting to press our luck any further, this was our last effort on behalf of the hospital.

During the time of our tunneling and hospital operations, I was frequently walking along Marszalkowska Street. On one occasion, I ran into a small group of scared, lonely children, about 10 to 12 years old, without their parents. I admonished them for being on the street. They told me their parents had left the house to find food and never returned. While talking with them I spotted, passing by, my close friend Wanda Czechowska, who upon seeing this unusual situation offered her help. Without much ado, I took the children to an empty movie theatre nearby on Marszalkowska Street. Suddenly, I noticed a big bomb lodged in the ceiling of the theatre's main room which luckily hadn't exploded. First, however, I asked Wanda to check in the nearby apartments to get blankets and anything else we could use. Opening the door, I found two more children crying and very scared. I immediately realized I was facing a problem of major proportions. So, Wanda and I started going to nearby buildings and knocking on doors to see if more children were stranded. Within 30 minutes, we found at least 10 more children in a similar state, all cold and hungry. I took them all to the theater and asked a kindly Wanda to look after them until it could be decided what to do. I was able to collect other children until we had about 20 of them gathered at the theater. The only thing I could give them was water and a few crackers I had with me. Later we moved them safely, in the company of some civilians, to the town of Pruszkow not far from Warsaw, where there was a temporary refugee camp.

Before the war, my friend Wanda was a swimming champion of Poland (I did not remember in what category or class). As we met she complained to me without any embarrassment about her extremely dirty smelling body, which she could not abide anymore. I suggested she go to my apartment, which was open, pull out from hiding a small wood stove, and use wood and coal stored in the kitchen. In the meantime I would bring a bucket of water from the outside, as there was none in the apartment. In this way she would be able to wash herself in hot water and also wash her clothes. The latter would dry quickly with the wood stove providing much heat. We acted accordingly. I also washed myself and changed my clothes, a real rarity. Then I boiled some water, made tea and took out the remaining piece of hidden gingerbread from the kitchen cabinet and offered it to Wanda. That's all there was to eat. We were truly happy, fresh and clean and no longer hungry. Wanda declared, "Janek, I am so very happy and grateful for the gift I received from you in these dramatic times, which presumably no other woman could receive." We talked for a little while about what she was doing presently, about the incredible famine, lack of arms and ammunition and agreed that, under the circumstances, we would probably have to surrender soon. We left the building, and very warmly said good-bye to each other. This was the last time I saw Wanda in my life.

My next plan was to go to the Maltanski Hospital, where Barbara Natorff-Tokarczyk and Zbyszka Sikorska were working. Before this, however, I decided to return and check on my neighbor living in an apartment across from mine. She was a pianist. Unfortunately, during the uprising I did not see her at all, which worried me. I found the apartment open and this time around she still was not there. In her living room stood a large old piano, and on the right was a large box which caught my eye. Intrigued I decided to open it up and, to my surprise, it was full to the brim with cigarettes. I left, hid in her sofa, about 100 of them for her own use and packed the rest into my backpack. I thought it would be a good idea to give them to the fighting soldiers. I went close to the front line and distributed them among the soldiers to their great joy. Thereafter I returned to my apartment and to my surprise I ran into my lady-pianist neighbor. I told her what I had done with her cigarettes and asked her not to be angry with me since the cigarettes were used for a worthy purpose. She looked at me, smiled, and said that if the cigarettes made the soldiers happy she was happy too.

Two days later, I ran into a Polish army defensive line and recognized Lieutenant Kazimierz Czarkowski—"Luty." His platoon of soldiers had brought in a *Volksdeutsche* Polish lady into their position. The men wanted to execute her, but the lieutenant ordered them to let her go. He explained to me that while being chased by a German patrol, he ran into a building and up to a fourth floor apartment with the door slightly ajar. "I pushed the door open and called for help. This same woman came to the door and allowed me to come in. Not only that, she hid me in a wardrobe cabinet and covered me with clothes. Within minutes German soldiers reached the fourth floor and began banging on apartment doors. When they came to her apartment, she told them no one was there, but they started to push their way in. She threw a fit, all in good German, and finally coaxed them to leave. So you see, she simply saved my life. I can't do anything to her." This proved to be yet another episode of bravery and luck.

Without a new order or task, I decided to return again to the Maltanski Hospital where my good friend Dr. Zbyszka Sikorska worked, one of the head surgeons, as well as a very young surgeon, code name "Basia"— Barbara Natorff-Tokarczyk, my future wife. Both of them were doing their best to help all the wounded. One of the patients I personally saw was a young man whose skin was dramatically burned by an incendiary bomb. One of the doctors told me that this young surgeon "Basia" received a

Polish Underground Army armbands worn by Jan and Barbara during the 1944 uprising.

high award because in the course of an operation on the burn victim she was wounded herself when the Germans attacked the hospital. Notwithstanding, she continued with the surgery to the end, saving the young soldier.

I again offered my services. The doctor pleaded with me to risk another foraging attempt to the Polish army facility. So at the risk of being court-martialed by a raging colonel, I returned to the scene of my crime. Facing me was the colonel I had assaulted earlier. Words almost stuck in my throat, but I managed, "Good morning, sir, I've come to collect more medical supplies." To my astonishment, he replied, "Take what you need and take it to the hospital." Before he could change his mind, we moved quickly to load our packs and leave. Back at the hospital, I told the doctor what had transpired at the storage building. This prompted him to write out a second note of appreciation, which I pocketed and eventually lost. In any event, my good name was established with the doctor-in-charge and the staff. Little did I know then that they would return the favor by helping me become a prisoner of war and escape the Soviet invasion of Poland.

One night into the second month of the uprising, Allied bombers

Armbands depicted over a picture of the uprising battle with German occupiers, 1944.

flew over Warsaw to make a supply airdrop. As luck would have it, only half of the parachuted crates landed in Polish-controlled areas. Also to our frustration, much of the ammunition was mismatched to the weapons used by the AK. What we didn't know at the time was that the bombers were crewed by Poles who had taken off from airfields in Italy. Senior Soviet Army commanders had refused to grant permission for the aircraft to operate from much closer Russian-controlled fields. Some crews had come from as far as South Africa, where they had been welcomed with citizenship and assimilation. The South African reception for fighting Poles was extended for Polish military action with the British Eighth Army in the defeat of the German Afrika Korps at Tobruk in North Africa. Later in London, I met a former Polish pilot who told me they approached Warsaw without using navigational aids, as they could see the flames of the burning city from miles away. To his deepest regret, they were of little help to the resistance on the ground.

One of the most demoralizing experiences during the uprising were the atrocities perpetrated on the Polish people by non–German forces under SS command. Ukrainians, whose hatred of Poles was paramount and who were recruited to SS-command units, wrought a special hell on the streets. One such formation was the 14th Waffen-SS Galizien Division commanded by Ukrainian general Vlassov. We were informed that Vlassov was not in Warsaw, but that elements of his division were. These elements forced women and children to walk in front of their tank formations. As they approached AK defensive positions at intersections, AK gunners were able to fire into the sides of the tanks, causing just enough of a diversion to allow the captive Poles to escape down a side street. In one incident, I was waiting nearby and able to gather up several of them and get them safely to the movie theater. The children were starving, but we had no food to give them, only temporary shelter until the danger passed.

In a similar scene on a Warsaw street, a Polish soldier observed German tanks approaching Kilinski Square. Thirteen- and fourteen-year-olds were throwing petrol-filled bottles and managed to set fire to a tank almost every time. On the 18th, the Germans deliberately left a tank loaded with explosives in the square. Our boys had no idea. When they approached it, there was an explosion causing many deaths, especially amongst the youngsters. Hatred of these villains grew with every atrocity. They would round up Poles and place them in front of tanks, so that the insurgents wouldn't shoot. It was a ghastly sight: you couldn't fire at your own, and it was even worse to see the bastards pressing on ahead. They would kill the poor wretches, despite sustaining many casualties themselves. That's how it was on Leszno Street, where both the hostages and the tank and its crew were destroyed. The Germans often went through a routine of running over several dozen hostages at a time with their tanks (Davies, p. 299).

As the end of September approached, I could sense the ebbing of the resolve to fight to the end at all echelons of the resistance. The means to carry on the fight — food, medicine, weapons and ammunition — were all but expended. I felt it even within myself. I wondered how many more times I would be allowed to escape capture or death in the streets. This occasionally would strike me to the bone. I remember how once, while moving carefully along Marszalkowska Street, I let my guard down. I stopped to talk to a Polish army lieutenant, not older than myself. His makeshift uniform was covered with dirt and grime, but his eyes were bright and shining with the hope of survival. We shook hands as we parted and, at that moment, he was felled by a sniper's bullet to his upper chest. I reached down and checked his pulse and found that he was dead before he hit the ground. I had no time to spot the sniper, as I pulled his body into a nearby doorway. I moved further into the building and on to a staircase to the basement. Just then I saw a German train on a rail line across the street. A crew serving an artillery piece on a flatbed car had loaded a round into the breech and fired at the building. I was blown down into the cellar, but fortunately not hurt other than a slight concussion. After lying still for a few minutes, I staggered out a rear door and headed to the Maltanski Hospital. There was nothing I could do with the lieutenant's body as I hadn't the strength to carry him from the building. I could only hope someone could give him a decent burial.

As I made my way back once again to the hospital, I was passing a storefront with a large glass display window. A shell, just missing me, shattered the window, spraying shards of glass all over me. Fortunately, my eyes were spared. I had acquired a German army tunic from a dead soldier a few days earlier and the strong material helped prevent more numerous cuts. At the hospital, Dr. Zbyszka Sikorska and Dr. Barbara Natorff-Tokarczyk extracted the glass with a surgical instrument and cleaned several skin wounds, and all the while I was cursing Hitler and Stalin. Russian propaganda was already declaring that Poland had been sold at the Yalta conference and that Poland would become a Russian state. So, as I look back, I think now that all of the past months were boiling up inside me at that moment. Whatever I had to say in my disjointed way didn't impress Barbara. She told me to stop cursing, it was not helping anything.

While at the hospital, word came of our army's surrender to the German command in Warsaw headed by SS General Erich von dem Bach in the early morning hours of October 3. Our hungry soldiers could no longer fight with nothing. We all knew it was coming, but it stunned us nevertheless. As I made ready to leave the hospital, I walked out to the front of the entrance with Zbyszka. Just then, a German command car with six men in it pulled up to the hospital. I quickly decided this would be a good time to remove my AK armband and stuff it in my pocket. The senior officer, a colonel, identified himself in a somewhat formal manner, then declared that the hospital would be completely dismantled and transported to Germany. He didn't know where yet, but those were his immediate orders. He seemed in a hurry and, as it turned out, he was. He made it clear that the Red Army was already approaching from the east, so it was time to move with all haste. I don't know whether other hospitals in Warsaw were subjected to what really was their destruction, but the German policy of performing the same "extractions" of select factories had been pursued since the beginning of the occupation. The orders given to Governor Frank were to strip Poland of its economic infrastructure. Zbyszka, as a skilled surgeon who had provided emergency operations on Germans, was well known to them, so this may have helped to attract their attention to this hospital — that plus the fact the hospital had survived serious damage during the war. Whatever had prompted their order to take possession of the hospital, it also presented us with a life-altering choice: remain in Warsaw to confront the Russians or become prisoners of war in Germany. For me, and ultimately Barbara, it meant a new life, but a life far away from our native Poland. I cried unashamedly when the Germans lowered the Polish flag in front of the hospital. It was the most horrible and devastating moment of my life.

CHAPTER 11

Prisoners of War

As emotional an occasion as it was, the arrival of the German colonel and his men proved to be almost surreal. At times the colonel's orders for removal of the hospital — down to the foundation — and transport of patients took on the tones of discussion, rather than commands. They had some food with them — fresh bread and cooked ham — which they shared with the doctors and some of the patients. I had to admit, it was delicious, especially compared to the stale fare we all had been living on for the past two months. We were not treated as captured prisoners. There were no arrests or detentions. As I look back, there wasn't time for that. The advancing Red Army was very much on their minds, as it was on ours.

The colonel told the medical staff that they would accompany the dismantled hospital to its new location in Germany. Again, this seemed to be a directive of sorts and not a military order, which in reality it was. The doctors, nurses and orderlies all seemed to accept their fate without resistance or protest. This included Zbyszka and Barbara. Patients who were unable to walk would be allowed to go to Germany for further treatment and recuperation. Patients who were mobile, the walking wounded, would remain in Warsaw. Zbyszka, being the forceful woman she was, decided to insist that I be included in the patient list. The colonel's immediate reaction was less than positive. She pleaded that I would be executed by the Russians, that I was on a blacklist with the NKVD, and must escape. When the colonel said that I was not at all wounded, Zbyszka quickly replied, "I will make him wounded!" She then explained that they would make a leg cast and give me crutches. That gave the colonel pause, but he relented and allowed me to become a patient. In retrospect, I believe the colonel and other Germans looked on me simply as a nuisance and a distraction from their duties. Fortunately, however, that did not cause them to exclude me from boarding the train to whatever fate lay ahead.

123

It took most of a month to dismantle the hospital and load it on a train that had been pulled into a rail siding a short distance away. Since we were not yet in a lock-down prisoner status, I decided to return to my apartment that first afternoon and alert my mother to my eminent departure. She was not there that day and had still not returned the next morning. I started a search for her, and then word came that large numbers of Polish women had been rounded up and sent to a camp in the village of Pruszkow, just outside Warsaw. I left a note for her, and then gathered up a few things to take with me. On the way out the door, I went back and picked up one memento of my childhood — a small stuffed rabbit — to make the journey with me. As if she had read my mind, Barbara also returned to her home to collect some items, among them a stuffed monkey. There was no one there. Her father, Henryk Tokarczyk, had been sent to a concentration camp, Sachsenhousen in Oranienburg near Berlin, and her mother, Zofia Natorff-Tokarczyk, to a labor camp in Dickholzen near Hildesheim, both in Germany. Rabbit and monkey somehow survived a long journey from Germany through the POW camps to Italy. Somehow they were sent on to England, then to their final destination in the U.S. From Chicago they came with us to Boulder, Colorado, and are now

Jan and Barbara's childhood stuffed animals, his rabbit and her monkey, both survivors of the war.

resting comfortably on my library desk. Their presence is a constant reminder of our journey from Warsaw.

On the way back to the hospital, I decided to stop by the apartment of Jerzy Czechowicz, my close friend and classmate. I had in mind to get my hands on Jerzy's fine 1776 bottle of fermented honey, or mead, as it is known in Polish, for the trip to Germany. I had mentioned my intention to bring along some rare liquor, to which the Germans said, "Fine, bring it here and we'll all have a drink." Jerzy was there, as was the bottle. When I told Jerzy of the plans I had set in motion to escape the Russians, I was able to convince him to join us, subject to selling it to the German officer-in-charge. On our way back walking along Marszalkowska Street, we spotted an apartment burning and no people in sight. We entered the building and found no one there. My eyes were drawn to an elegant oil painting in a gilded frame. It looked to be worth rescuing, so I carried it out to the entrance of the building, wrote the apartment address on the back and hoped that it might be returned to the owner. When we arrived at the hospital, the bottle of mead in hand, a collective decision was made to have a party. The doctors joined us, as did a few German soldiers, which made yet another surreal occasion with our captors. The mead produced clearer minds, but paralyzed the legs. The next day, I was fitted for a leg

Drawing by Barbara "Basia" Natorff-Tokarczyk of the hospital-prisoner train arriving at the Zeithain POW camp.

cast and given a pair of crutches, so my mobility was reduced to remaining close to the hospital and sleeping in a train boxcar that would carry some of us to Germany.

As the work of dismantling the hospital was being completed, it was time to make what little preparations we could for the trip to Germany. We were fortunate in quietly assimilating Jerzy into the hospital staff. He was a gifted linguist and his fluency in both German and Russian would come in handy in the challenges we would all face. I was able to talk the Germans into giving us a generous supply of hay for three boxcars that would be occupied by the hospital staff and patients. The hay would help to keep us warm and more comfortable than sleeping on the hard board floor. I still wore the German army tunic and my school cap, which was not much protection against the wind whipping inside the car. The Germans provided buckets for human waste and drinking water. Food, such as weak soup and bread, would be given to us during refueling stops. Zbyszka and Barbara were in another boxcar, but Jerzy and I were together. I did not know it at the time, but there was a second train carrying equipment and staff from other hospitals in the Warsaw area. All in all, over 1,000 wounded Polish prisoners and over 200 doctors, nurses and aides were transported to Germany. It's hard to believe the disciplined German soldiers could have looked the other way, but as it turned out, children of some hospital staff members and family pets made it aboard the two evacuation trains.

Drawing by "Basia" of the Zeithain POW camp's outer perimeter.

We departed on November 5, 1944. Before leaving, a German officer read an order declaring us prisoners of war and attached under control to a POW camp in Zeithain, Stalag IV B, where the hospital would again be set up. Stalag IV B was one of the largest prisoner of war camps in Germany during World War II. Stalag is abbreviation of the German *Stammlager* ("Main Camp"). It was located 0.5 mile northeast of the town of Mühlberg in Brandenburg, just east of the Elbe River and north of Dresden. The journey took eight days and we all managed to survive, except one young Polish woman who was a "nuisance patient" like me. Somehow a guard was agitated enough to shoot her while the train had stopped. When he and other soldiers reacted with laughter to the killing, I and others demanded to confer with a representative of the International Red Cross. As POWs, we were granted prisoner rights under the provisions of the Geneva Convention. Their laughter quickly stopped, but surprisingly a Swiss representative was called and took our complaint. The Germans denied it all, of course, and I doubt if anything was ever done. I had thought of escaping once underway, but the increasingly cold nights, lack of warm clothing, finding the right time to cut away the cast on my leg, and the distance to refuge in Switzerland made me return to reality. I simply would have frozen to death had I tried to escape.

Our survival on the prison train was, to be sure, a hardship, but it was bearable. The main concern we had was our health. We had no opportunity to bathe before leaving Warsaw, and other than a "bucket wash" we were in a near putrid state at the end of the journey. The other difficulty we had to sort out among the 15 or so men and women in the boxcar was privacy for the toilet and washing. We seemed to manage this after the first day or two of self-consciousness, then after that it became a daily routine.

Finally, in mid-afternoon of November 13, 1944, the steam locomotive pulled the train slowly into the station of Jacobsthal, which served what we now knew as the Zeithain Hospital Camp, Stalag 304. The event was later recorded in an ink drawing by Barbara "Basia" Natorff-Tokarczyk, my future wife. The drawing depicting the unloading of the wounded and sick patients was passed to me and remains with me as a reminder of our prisoner experience. After the sick and wounded were taken off the train, the walking medical staff and patients were herded together and led to a bath house. It was a joy simply to walk and exercise our limbs again. Some of us had not had a real bath for weeks, even a few months, so the evidence was obvious. The Germans were convinced we all were contaminated with lice, but that was not the case. It simply was accumulated filth. We were forced to strip naked outside — men and women together. The men all chose to look away from the women, giving them some decency of privacy before they entered the bath house. All our clothes were taken and put through a steam cleaning process then given back to us after we exited the bathhouse. Thus, I still had my German army tunic and "good luck" school hat.

Outside again, our guards — some of them unarmed — kept up yelling commands to the point of total incoherence and confusion. I tried to ask questions as to what was happening to us, but I was totally ignored. I even suggested to one guard standing by an opening to a fence that it would be a fine day for a walk, and what if I just kept walking out of the camp. By the look on his face, he either thought he misunderstood what I had said or chose to completely ignore me. We were then led to a section of at least 20 barracks that had been designated for Polish prisoners. This section was a camp within the main camp, and we Poles had to enter the main camp through our own front gate. One German officer welcomed us with the comment that hundreds of Russian prisoners had died in these same barracks. We were also told that as many as 5,000 Russians died at Zeithain. We were herded into the barracks randomly, men and women together, but then a few days later we were separated.

Up to 40 persons were housed in each barracks. There was one small woodstove, which an officer told us we were not allowed to use. With winter coming on, this would become the center of our first conflict with our keepers. Toilets were outside the barracks and we took it upon ourselves to arrange separate facilities for men and women. The beds were crudely made and the mattresses, consisting of hay stuffed in gunnysacks, were alive with hundreds of bedbugs, all fat and nasty. So our first task, which lasted the remainder of the day and nearly all night, was to pick out and burn the bed bugs.

Ignoring the command not to use the stove, we took some wood slats from the beds and started a fire. Within minutes, an officer charged into the barracks and demanded to know how we were able to start a fire and where we got the wood and matches. Jerzy and I tried to explain that we found both in the barracks. The officer screamed, "No, that's impossible!" We continued to argue to the point I think we wore him down. He issued his final order to put the fire out, and to put all lights out so the camp could not be spotted for night bombing by the Americans. Judging this to be ridiculous, we proceeded to disobey by letting the fire burn and covering the windows so that we could continue "Operation Bed Bug."

We did have one further discussion with the officer, over food rations. Again, I ended up speaking out. I told him that we had not eaten that day and asked for his help. He told us to appoint one among us to bring in

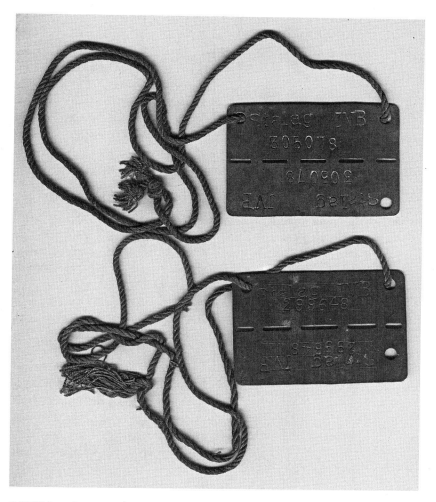

POW Identification tags issued to Jan and Barbara Rosinski at the Zeithain Camp, Germany, 1944.

what food was available — there was no separate mess hall — and that person would be allowed to have one extra piece of bread each day for this extra duty. I took it upon myself to appoint the biggest man among us, who would need extra nourishment, to be our food provider. He was very thankful, and thus I had my first loyal subordinate. Not much fortune was with us for that first meal, as were given only dark bread, margarine and water. Still plagued with hunger, few if any of us slept that night. Thus ended our first day at Stalag 304. The next day, with German efficiency, we were issued prisoner ID tags to be hung around our necks by a string. Barbara's tag was marked with her name and number, 299648 Block

IV B, and mine with name and number, 305078 Block IV B. They remain in our possession and are the only reminder, other than our memories, of our prisoner experience.

Zeithain would be our place of incarceration for the next five months. Having escaped the invasion of the Red Army in Warsaw, we would have yet another opportunity to be "liberated" by Poland's arch enemy disguised throughout the war years as our ally. We all sought normalcy in our daily lives, and to a certain extent we achieved that collectively. The operation of the "Polish Army Hospital" became the center of our existence. The medical equipment and supplies off-loaded from the train were installed in a building adjacent to our barracks area. Soon its reputation for impartial treatment for all who came for medical treatment, including the German military contingent, was widely recognized throughout the entire camp. Our doctors and nurses made it known to all who entered that everyone was entitled to the same professional care.

Since both Barbara and Zbyszka spoke acceptable German, it is likely they attracted more German patients than did others on the medical staff. This helped pave the way for improved access to food supplies, but there remained days when we became desperate for basic food. More than a few times we were forced to collect grass to boil for a soup. Potatoes were always a luxury, as were any vegetables that could be obtained from farms outside the camp. Even one of our doctor's pet dog was not exempt from becoming a source of badly needed protein. Our complaints to the camp commandant and other Germans generally fell on deaf ears. On one occasion, we told them, "If you want to starve us, why don't you just be done with it and shoot us!" A German officer replied, "That is not a matter for jokes." "Of course it isn't," we agreed. "We are starving while providing medical help to everyone who comes to the hospital." Finally, after a month, a canteen, offering some improvement in food, was set up in the hospital building for the medical staff.

Boldly telling the Germans of my background in physics and chemistry, I talked my way into becoming the head of the X-ray department. This, in turn, allowed me occasional access to the canteen and thus another source for an improved diet. The medical staff, as well as Polish officers and noncommissioned officers, were not required to do heavy labor. I was considered a noncommissioned officer, so I was not put on any work details. In one instance, however, I actually volunteered for a distasteful job. We discovered the bodies of 10, possibly more, bodies of Russian soldiers in a building close to our sector. To prevent the spread of disease from the decomposed bodies I volunteered to organize a small burial detail.

The guards carried the bodies to an open field that had become a cemetery and we dug individual graves for these nameless men.

Undoubtedly, the most welcome event was the arrival of the first Red Cross packages after the third week in the camp. It turned out the first delivery, we were told, was of so-called half-packages. Later, every six weeks or so, we would receive a regular package that contained canned food, processed meats, cheese, candies, crackers and cigarettes. They were all packaged and supplied from Switzerland. Fortunately, I did not smoke, so I was able to trade cigarettes, valued more than reichsmarks, as a currency for extra food. I did quite well in my little horde of food, especially eggs, the most highly regarded commodity. I also sold my Swiss watch to a guard for two eggs, which I boiled and gave to Barbara. She was not eating well and I was worried about her health and resistance to disease in the hospital. The Red Cross also aided the prisoners by providing mail service to and from the camp. Through their assistance, I was able to locate and communicate with my mother in a labor camp in Pruszkow, Poland.

The first visit of International Red Cross representatives to the camp had nothing to do with food packages. As a German guard had shot one of our nurses without provocation, we immediately demanded an appeal to the Red Cross, and to our amazement, our keepers complied. Within a few days, Red Cross representatives arrived to conduct an investigation. The camp commandant went through the motions of cooperation, but refused to make the guard available for questioning. Even though nothing came of the incident, the camp guards became more circumspect in their conduct towards us. Eventually, a number of us were allowed to go outside the camp to the nearby village of Strehla and one other village to collect food and small items needed for maintenance for the hospital. I would occasionally go with Barbara and Zbyszka, and we were always greeted with courtesy by village shopkeepers. In fact, as we were identified as medical staff to the locals, we rarely were asked for payment. Such was yet another dichotomy of our existence in the land of our captors. These brief trips outside the camp gave rise to devising ways of escape. Our objective would have been neutral Switzerland. However, with oncoming cold weather we would not have survived.

We were able to follow some of the major events of the war from BBC broadcasts on a radio that was kept hidden in one of the barracks. To prevent its discovery by the guards, one person was appointed to monitor the news at set times each day and pass the latest reported developments to a contact in each barracks. By early spring, it was clear to all of us that the Wehrmacht was in full retreat on both Eastern and Western fronts. As

April arrived, fewer and fewer guards and other German personnel were seen in the camp. Soon we could see that chaos was beginning to reign as more of our keepers silently disappeared. No announcement was made by the Germans that the camp was being abandoned. It was just happening day by day and hour by hour. There was a small group of Russian prisoners, perhaps as many as 40 or 50, who had uncovered a store of vodka. They had now become a drunken mob, demanding access to the hospital. I had to admit we were afraid of them, especially if they got their hands on any weapons. The time had come to act and take control of the security of the camp. It was April 23, 1945.

We were not well organized for collective action in our sector of the camp. Actually, we weren't organized at all. We had not elected or appointed a leader, so occasionally I stepped in to resolve disputes or organize ourselves when a team effort was required. With the camp now all but abandoned by our guards, I decided that we needed to take over the guard towers and the mounted machine guns at each tower. My friend Maczek from Warsaw took one of the towers and I volunteered myself for a tower

Jan Rosinski as a prisoner in the Zeithain POW camp.

at the front entrance of the camp. It proved to be a problem just climbing up the crude ladder, which was covered with barbed wire. My hands and arms became bloodied, which took me back to the hospital later in the day. My more immediate problem, however, was trying to figure out how to operate the machine gun and, if necessary, pull the pin on grenades stored in a box. While immersed in this puzzle, the telephone in the tower rang. In an excited voice, Maczek told me, "I have the guard who killed our nurse!" "Well, hold him," I replied, "I'll be there in just a few minutes."

Just then, I looked up to see an approaching German army column in the distance. What a mess! Here I am in a key defensive position, fumbling with these damn weapons and now facing overwhelming numbers of the enemy. The only thing I could do was to at least look alert and ready. The German convoy was headed right to the camp's front gate and the tower. Most of the soldiers were on foot and marching in good order. It looked to be a battalion size unit or what had once been a battalion. At the head of the column was a small command car, with a senior officer seated next to the driver. As the car pulled up to the gate, the officer stood up and called out: "This is a Waffen SS unit and we are headed west to Halle to surrender to the Americans there. Do I have your permission to pass through the camp?" The camp was on the most direct route west, so it seemed a logical request. What choice did I have? I told him, "The gate is unlocked, you may pass through." He saluted, and as they moved through the gate, I called out, "How far away are the Russians?" He replied, "Two hours and headed in this direction."

Looking back at the incident, I now wonder why I didn't think of collecting a few of us and simply following the Germans the few miles to Halle and freedom. It would have been a full day's walk, if we were not intercepted by the Russian advance. However, I wanted to see that captured guard. When I called Maczek back and told him I was on my way, he said they had already executed him. The chosen method was dropping him headfirst from one of the towers. Maczek would have made a good professional soldier, but through correspondence with him in later years, I learned that he had become a successful medical doctor. The SS officer proved to be accurate in the timing of the Red Army's arrival. But it wasn't at all what we had expected. As the low thundering noise and formation drew nearer, it wasn't tanks and trucks, but the famous, or perhaps infamous, depending on where one stood, Russian Cossacks.

CHAPTER 12

The Russians Arrive
and We Escape

The SS officer was not far wrong on the arrival of the Red Army, and the reason for his apparent sense of urgency to reach the American lines would soon become clear to me. I had left everything behind in Warsaw — family, friends and a beginning professional life — to escape the Russians. Now they were upon us again. Rumbling out of the east came a gaggle of what looked to be about 100 Cossack riders heading straight for the camp. In appearance, they fulfilled all that had been told about them. To a man, and some women, they were the shaggiest and dirtiest human beings I had ever laid eyes on. Their mounts — small sturdy Siberian ponies — easily fit the same description. They all were traveling light. No large packs, just machine guns or rifles looped over their shoulders and backs, as was ammunition bandoliers. Their water bags, as it turned out, contained more alcohol — a fermented milky liquid or vodka — than water. The women riders among them were perhaps even more fearful. Only the bandoliers covered their huge bare breasts. Their dress, such as it was, consisted only of leather pants and boots.

As they rode into the camp, they immediately dismounted and began walking all over the camp. They were clearly drunk, or well on their way. One of their apparent leaders came toward me, speaking a language that I could not understand. Even Jerzy, who spoke fluent Russian, could not understand a word. For certain, it was not Russian. The leader became impatient when he could not understand me, but then offered me a drink from his "water bag." I could see that my refusal was agitating him, so down my gullet it went. It was a fermented liquid of some sort and beyond drinkable. Quickly, their attention turned to foraging in the camp for women as well as food. Some of the Cossack women stripped their clothes off completely and appeared to be offering sex to some of us men. We could not understand them, of course, so we tried to move away from their immediate presence.

A crisis loomed ahead, at least for the six hours or so the Cossacks remained in the camp before riding off to harass yet another fallen foe. We alerted the women on the hospital staff to lock and barricade themselves in the building. Barbara and Zbyszka were among them. While we were able to protect most of them for those terrifying hours, a few were caught and raped. We were also harassed by a band of 30 to 40 Russian prisoners roaming the camp after finding a liquor supply. Later in the day, a motorized infantry unit of regular Russian troops arrived. We immediately alerted them to the attacks on the women. We found three or four Cossacks who had taken two Polish women, one with her dress torn off. Without a word, the Russian officer drew his pistol and shot two of the Cossacks. The atmosphere of fear quickly changed, and the Cossacks mounted their ponies and rode off to the west. Looking back at this terrifying experience, it seems as though the Red Army was using the Cossacks as shock troops, and that Russian commanders knew very well what was occurring with these advance elements of their army. Perhaps it was a form of payback for the dangers and hardships the Cossacks had endured in previous campaigns against the *Wehrmacht* in Russia. So, this is how we were "liberated" by the Red Army.

The next day, a contingent of Russian soldiers and officers arrived at the camp. I was sitting on a small mound of a hill not far from the front gate as their vehicles came to a stop near me. One officer, with obvious authority, strode toward me, and demanded, "Who are you, and what are you?" In my basic Russian, I gave him my name and Polish identity. Interestingly, he identified himself as Major Leontiev of the Soviet NKVD. This was the People's Commissariat for Internal Affairs, the secret police of the Soviet Union and predecessor to the KGB, the Committee for State Security. His duty at the camp, we were to learn, was to interrogate and process the remaining Russian prisoners, to determine those who would be allowed to reintegrate into the army and those to be condemned to labor camps or worse. In the meantime, Leontiev said that any Germans they captured would all be hanged. We Poles, however, were not outside his periphery of suspicion as what he described as "enemies of the Soviet Union." "Well," I said, "that's probably true. However, the war is over, so we will now belong to Russia. But, we would still like to go back and rebuild Poland." He merely grunted, and that brought an end to our brief conversation.

After two days passed, it became clear that the Russians would not impose tight security in the camp. Although Russian soldiers were moving in and out of the area, they did not post guards over us. The front gate was also left unlocked on most days, more for their convenience for coming and going than for us. They also made some effort to requisition local sources of food for us, which usually meant stealing or confiscating whatever they could find from nearby farms and villages. On one occasion they killed a cow and made a delicious beef soup — at least at the time it seemed tasty. They also provided other meat by herding up some sheep and machine gunning them. Another unexpected addition was barrels of army vodka. It smelled like kerosene, but it was vodka, industrial grade at that. Then for a nonfood item it was Russian army women looking for sexual adventure outside their ranks and overlooked by their officers. While most of the Russian men were of average size, it seemed as though the women were huge, and especially their breasts. Some in their revelry wore stolen German clothes, while some were virtually naked. All were drunk. Under these circumstances we Polish men would have eventually faced serious trouble if we had been stupid enough to accommodate them. Their weapons were nearby, and all it would take would be an insult or misunderstanding to spark a serious incident.

Soon enough we had almost complete freedom of movement within the camp. Later during that first week under the Russians, I decided to go to Major Leontiev's office, which was located on a small hill overlooking the main camp. I asked for permission to go to the village of Strehla two or three kilometers away to bargain for some food. After questioning me to his satisfaction, he told me I could go directly and return directly. As I was walking along the road, I was stopped by a Russian patrol and taken in their jeep to a nearby jail. I was shoved into the presence of a colonel, who appeared drunk and who would stay drunk for most of the week they kept me locked up. At this first encounter, he boasted proudly that while his father was a worker, "I became a colonel, and this could only happen in the Soviet Union." "Well, that's true," I said, "but can't you let me go so that I can return to our hospital?" "No, we need to know what you are doing out here." I explained several times the simple truth that I had Major Leontiev's permission to buy some food in the village. It didn't matter, as they kept asking me the same questions over and over.

There was a young woman in a cell next to mine who was interrogated daily and treated very harshly. In fact, I froze in disbelief as she was raped every day that I was there. We were able to speak in English, and she told me she was Dutch and had been falsely arrested as a spy. She died after being molested the day before my release from the jail. That occurred when the colonel appeared to have lost interest in me and ordered me to report back to the camp to Major Leontiev. My inconvenience didn't seem to interest the major, so that ended that incident.

What this incident did do, however, was to energize me to begin planning for an escape to an allied zone of occupation. In fact, every single person in the Polish camp was now thinking along the same lines. I was approached any number of times with some outlandish ideas. Some were thinking of organizing several of us and simply marching out of the camp to Warsaw. Others schemed to steal a truck and race for the allied lines. I purposely declined such offers or ideas, mostly because of all the loose talk going around the camp. I decided to organize my own small group, with the objective of being the first to escape. I was certain there would be no opportunity for a second or third group to follow, as the Russians would quickly lock the camp down. As it turned out, that is exactly what happened. So, I drew into my escape conspiracy Barbara, Jerzy Czechowicz, our Russian linguist, Zbyszka Sikorska and a fourth, Wojciech Krynicki. Over the next two or three days the pieces of the plan were put together. Our objective was the same as the Waffen SS unit that had passed through the main camp more than two weeks ago — the American lines at Halle. We needed to recruit the help of a Russian soldier to get us bicycles on the outside to distance ourselves more rapidly from the camp, and darkness, without the camp lights, to cover our exit. Our concern was not only the lights inside the camp, but also the powerful searchlights that could project a beam over 100 meters in any direction.

I had spotted some time before a rather handsome Russian soldier by the name of Gruszka, which means "pear" in Russian. I decided to approach him by offering him some small items from my Red Cross package. Finally, I took the plunge by asking him if he ever thought of living in the West, such as in America. While I clearly had his attention, I told him I had an aunt and uncle in Chicago who might be able to help him, if he could help me. I wrote out their address for him. Without hesitating, he asked, "What would you like me to do?"

Mustering up all my courage, I asked, "Can you arrange to collect five bicycles and hide them outside the camp where we can find them?" I had planned on adding a fifth person to our group, but in the end, we remained four. "Also, we need to cut off the power to the searchlight. There's a transformer up the road in a locked shed. You will need to cut the lock off the door and replace it with a new lock. But before you do that, switch the transformer to the 'off' position." I gave him a metal saw blade I had sewn inside the back of my German army jacket for cutting the lock. At the time I hid the blade at home in Warsaw, I had no idea what it might be used for, but it seemed like something worthwhile to keep with me. If all went well, our escape would be on the next night. This was the crucial moment in our escape plan. Everything else had been made ready. We decided to travel under the contrived cover of being French, which might give us acceptance with the German civilian population and possibly dupe any Russian army elements we might run into. All of us except me spoke acceptable French, and we had sewn small homemade French flags on the front of our jackets. The only things we could carry with us were small pieces of bread and other food items in each of the rucksacks we carried on our backs. Barbara managed to squeeze in her stuffed monkey and I my stuffed rabbit. Both were "good luck" charms for our freedom. Sadly, it seems my lucky university hat was lost or misplaced in the camp.

Just over two weeks after the Russians took control of the camp we stood ready to head for the main front gate, hoping it would be open. Gruszka, our Russian accomplice, made his way to the transformer shed but had difficulty maneuvering the control switch to the off position. There was nothing we could do but postpone our escape to the following night. As I recall, Jerzy went up to the shed to make sure he could identify the switch lever and tell Gruszka how to move it to the off position. We thus faced another 24 hours in the camp, raising the risk that our escape would somehow be revealed to other Poles in the camp, and then leak out to the Russians. In our desperation to sabotage the lights, we also attempted to shoot a terminal box on the power line, but we failed at that. Gruszka volunteered to try for a lucky shot, as did I, but we both failed. We were only able to take this risk because there was always sporadic rifle or pistol firing in the camp from drunken soldiers.

Having survived that danger, the next night at about 8:00 P.M., we walked one by one close to the front gate. This time Gruszka was successful in throwing the transformer switch off. He came back and that was the last we were to see of him. I thanked him for all he had done and hoped that we would meet again. Our parting was not without emotion. I could only hope that he survived any suspicion of what the Russians would consider as "traitorous acts." With heart in hand, I moved to open the gate latch and, thankfully, it was unlocked. Our way to freedom was open. It took us less than 10 minutes to find the bicycles behind some trees and underbrush and push off. I had never been a practiced bicycle rider, so Jerzy took the lead. The route we planned was first to head in an easterly direction, knowing that any Russian search parties sent out would almost certainly cover routes to the allied lines in the west.

We had ridden only a short distance when all hell broke loose in the camp. It was apparent that the camp command had detected some unidentified breach in security. Having failed to turn on the camp lights from the control in the camp headquarters building, they likely headed to the transformer station only to find it locked with no key to open it. All this commotion only spurred us to ride on at a faster pace. Fortunately, we were not followed. We rode still in a generally easterly direction for the next four hours. In passing through a forested area, we saw several signs warning of buried land mines, so we rode in single file to lessen the risk of riding over a mine. Later, when we passed by a clearing, we stopped to take in a most eerie sight. Silhouetted by a partially moonlit sky were two parked Messerschmitt ME-109 fighter aircraft that appeared to be in operating condition. Our imaginations immediately leaped to the possibilities of flying to the allies. Of course, this was only a passing dream. Barbara actually had a pilot's license, but she would have been overwhelmed in any attempt to get that relatively sophisticated aircraft off the ground. So, we rode on.

As midnight approached, we spotted a farm not far off the road. If the family would allow us, their barn would be a welcome place for a night's rest. At this point we were still running on adrenaline and nearly exhausted. We didn't want to sleep in the barn without permission, as, who knows, we might get shot. So I approached the darkened house and knocked loudly on the front door. The farmer opened the door cautiously, as Jerzy explained our situation — that we were French — and said we needed only to sleep a while before making off again on our way to Paris. The story sold, as our host led us to the barn and the loft, which had enough hay to make a resting place for the four of us. After a dead sleep, we woke with the sun and prepared to continue our journey, this time heading back westward towards Halle and the Allies. We felt fairly sure at that point that the Russians were not out searching for us. Without our asking, the farmer's wife offered us bread and milk, for which we were all thankful. I am certain they could not readily afford such generosity, but it was an act reflective of the true nature of German country folk that we had little chance to experience during our fortunately brief time there. (The generosity — compassion even — of the German shopkeepers in Strehla was another welcome experience.)

We had no compass and no one to guide us, other than the sun and the light of day to our backs as we headed west. A few hours later we crossed the Elbe River at Riesa without incident. We headed in a north-westerly direction that would take us around Dresden and on to the banks of the Saale River, a tributary of the Elbe and the last barrier before reaching the town of Halle, now occupied by the Allies. We had been nearly, at that point, ten hours on the road. In our shabby clothes we were able to blend in with the flow of refugees. No one paid us any attention. Jerzy and I did ask for directions from some Germans we passed, but the answers we got were more confusing than helpful. Finally, by late afternoon we reached the Saale. I thought that in an emergency we could attempt to swim across, as there was no bridge in sight. However, the water was too high and swift from the spring rains, so swimming was out of the question.

Hoping our luck would hold, we headed south downriver on a road that ran along the riverbank. Soon a vehicle and train bridge of some size loomed in the distance. However, also looming at the eastern end of the bridge was a squad of four or five Russian soldiers. This was a barrier we had not counted on. We reaffirmed among us that we would hold to the cover story that we were displaced French traveling home to Paris. I was the weak link in this story because I spoke little if any French. So I wrapped a scarf around my neck and took on the role of a sick man who could not talk.

We let Jerzy do the talking for us. As we approached the soldiers, Jerzy explained our situation and said that this route was the only way westward to France. The soldiers made no move to let us pass. One of them appeared to be a sergeant, and he told us that he could not let us pass without receiving a clearance from one of their officers. Jerzy protested we could not wait, that it was urgent for us to rest for the night in Halle, now in our sight. The sergeant said an officer would be coming soon, and we must wait. We all started talking among ourselves, trying to sow confusion on the scene, all the while slowly edging forward onto the bridge. We spotted three American soldiers, armed with tommy guns, at the other end of the bridge about fifty meters away, who were now attracted to our increasingly heated conversation with the Russians. We continued to walk slowly forward, but two of the Russians stayed with us, machine guns in hand. The senior American, a lieutenant, and his two men started walking toward us. Now it was as if everything was unfolding in slow motion. I thought to myself, *Now we have some fire power.* The lieutenant told us to continue walking slowly and follow him, even as one of the Russian soldiers demanded we wait for their officer to decide what to do with us. As we drew closer to the Americans, the three Americans intentionally turned their backs to us and the Russians and walked back to their post at the western end of the bridge. As we continued walking with our bicycles, the two Russians finally gave up at the midpoint on the bridge and returned to their post. The standoff was over. We had finally met our first Americans and reached freedom.

CHAPTER 13

With the British and the Polish Army

When we reached the end of the bridge, the lieutenant turned to us and asked if we were from the AK — the Home Army of Poland. I was astounded, not only that he might know of our identity, but also that he addressed me by my name and in excellent Polish. Obviously flustered, I acknowledged who we were as he shook my hand and welcomed us to the Allied zone. The wide grin on his face signaled that we were safe and among friends. I held his hand, it seemed, forever. All of us were simply giddy with joy. For the first time in memory, we were among normal, friendly people and, above all, safe. We were all so hungry and exhausted that we didn't have the mental capacity to question how they knew about our insignificant band of escapees. Yet, even today, I wonder what were the odds that in the midst of war-torn Germany we would meet first a Polish-American army officer. Later, we realized that the Russians at the Zeithain camp, and particularly NKVD Major Leontiev, in a raging fury, had alerted the Allied zone that we had escaped and had given our names, or at least my name, to the Americans.

The Russians had also requested that we be arrested and held for return to Zeithain. Almost laughingly, the lieutenant told us, "You know, to keep peace with the Russians, I should actually send you all back." "That will be the day!" I replied, and he laughed again. We also learned that the camp had been immediately locked down after our escape was discovered, making it impossible for the prisoners of the Polish Army Hospital to escape. Sometime later they were repatriated to Poland to live under a new Russian Communist-inspired regime.

The lieutenant, whose name I unfortunately cannot recall, informed us that since free Polish forces had entered the war under a British-coordinated command, we would be transferred to the British Eighth Army, which included the Second Polish Army. We stayed with the Americans for two days while the British made preparations to receive us. A bath and clean clothes were welcome luxury, as none of us had experienced either for an embarrassingly long time. Finally, after we had an emotional goodbye, two jeeps came and transported us 150 kilometers to a British camp in Northeim. This small city, at that time temporarily larger with the infusion of the British, is about 90 kilometers south of Hannover. We were welcomed openly and immediately provided with fresh British Army uniforms, without rank. Barbara, having small feet, could not find a fit in military shoes, so she was driven to a store in the town where a new pair of shoes were purchased. We were shown the mess facility and an empty barracks at the back of the camp, the luxury of showers included, which would be our home for the next two weeks. An army doctor gave us a physical exam and cautioned us to eat lightly since our digestive systems were not used to rich or plentiful food. I think he was surprised to learn that he was examining two physicians in Zbyszka and Barbara.

Most of our days were spent working with a debriefing team of intelligence men, who were intensely interested in all aspects of our underground experience in Warsaw and the German occupation. We cooperated fully and told them everything they wanted to know. It was the least we could do to establish a record of what we Poles endured through those bleak years. We learned that we would soon be transported to the Polish Second Army in Italy, a move we welcomed. In the meantime, I was assigned to a British Military Police company commanded by a 36-year-old Captain Davis. Barbara was given a temporary job at a medical field station. When I reported to Captain Davis, he told me, with a grin on his face, "Well, Jan, I think you're going to enjoy this job." He then assigned me to a control, or security, checkpoint to monitor all traffic on a major road passing the camp. There was a small guard shack there, and the station was equipped with a cross-bar for halting vehicles and persons for inspection. An MP armband and pistol came with the job. This pleased me no end, as finally I had some authority, however modest, and a little firepower to go with it.

That very first afternoon, a black Mercedes sedan approached the crossbar obstructing passage. As I looked in the car, there in the front passenger seat was Hilda, my German tennis partner from Katowice, an advocate for her glorious Third Reich. The driver was her husband, who had been identified to me as a Gestapo officer by the manager of the chemical plant where I worked in the summer of 1939. She recognized me in an obvious state of shock but gave no sign of knowing me. I decided, on the spur of the moment, to let them pass. Captain Davis was standing nearby and immediately approached me. He asked why I had let the car pass without inspection or questioning the passengers. I explained who they were and my belief that she probably knew of my involvement in the underground and chose not to report me to her husband. Davis didn't seem to be pleased with my decision. "Okay, that may be, but I don't have to be a gentleman. I'm ordering the car to be stopped." By that time it had entered the adjoining American sector.

The next day, I asked the captain if we could drive over to their sector and find out what had happened to them. He agreed and off we went in his jeep. We were astounded to learn from the American military police that they been put up in a luxury hotel. Now fully aware of the Gestapo identity of Hilda's husband, they explained that cooperation with such officers was becoming necessary in the event of war with Russia. A major

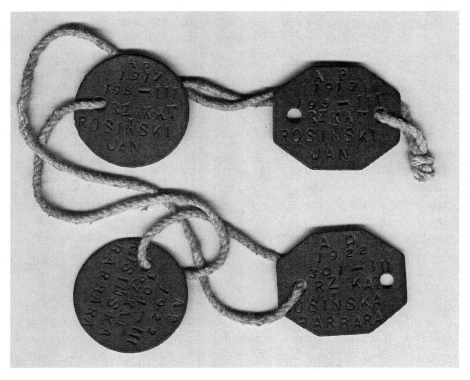

Polish Army dogtags issued to Jan and Barbara Rosinski, 1945.

told us, "These officers know everything about Russia and we know nothing. Our orders are to keep them alive and well fed. A war may never come, but we will have the people here whom we will need." We were unable to meet the two escapees, so we returned to our camp.

It may have not been the most romantic of moments, but knowing that both Barbara and I would be transported to the Polish Army zone of control in Italy, I asked, or perhaps told, her, "Well, since we will be traveling together, we should go as a married couple." Fortunately, she thought that an excellent idea; thus a marriage of 46 years came about, and not without considerable challenges and obstacles. We were able to find a Polish priest serving as an army chaplain who performed the ceremony on June 24, 1945. The marriage certificate recorded the names of three witnesses, and it was signed by Polish army chaplain (Captain) Stanislaw Paraszewski. He had been a prisoner of war in a camp in the Northeim area. The one suitable place for the ceremony was the makeshift officers club. However, arrangements there were complicated by the fact that Barbara, as a doctor, was an officer, while I was best described as a sergeant-officer candidate. Finally, it was settled that the ceremony would take place in the mess hall. Several well-wishers attended, including the commanding officer, who gave a short speech. One surprise was the appearance of Joe Bulhak, whom I had last seen on the streets of Warsaw. Joe apparently had taken on a new identity with British SID (Special Investigation Division). At the last minute, I was even able to buy a bouquet of flowers for Barbara. The day ended with a small gathering at a local restaurant. Barbara was a wonderful soul mate, and a moderating influence on my occasional outspokenness, particularly if it had anything to do with Hitler, Stalin and the Russians. At little more than five feet tall, with blond hair, blue eyes compassionate as a physician must be, and a radiant personality, she often was the sensible one in the family, as well as the problem solver.

Two days after the wedding, both Barbara and I received orders for transfer to the Polish Second Army headquarters in Ancona, Italy. Actually, the orders were more for her than for me. There was a priority need for surgeons at the army hospital there, and there was nothing more for us to do in Northeim. We were transported by car, with driver and armed escort, to Ancona via Munich and Verona. I think the "armed" part of the escort was a preventive measure against any misadventure in a newly defeated country. The four-day trip became our honeymoon of sorts. We had little money, so our accommodations along the way were timed for sleeping quarters in military facilities, and in Munich we stayed at the central YMCA.

My memory fails me here — that is, with our transfer to Polish forces in Italy. It seems we left behind our three other companions in our escape from Zeithain. They made their way back to Poland, as best as we knew. Jerzy Czechowicz returned with the intent to marry his fiancée and continue his education. Later, he worked many years at the Warsaw Institute of Technology as an assistant professor. We learned that, at the age of 57, he died in an accident while in the Tatra Mountains. Zbyszka Sikorska continued her medical career even under the prospect of a Soviet-dominated Communist regime. Most regrettably, we did not communicate with each other. Years later, Barbara and I received a telephone call from a relative in Warsaw that Zbyszka had died. No further explanation was given, other than that she had never married.

So our life started in the Adriatic city of Ancona. It is a city and port, with ferry and freighter routes going throughout the Baltic and Mediterranean areas. The midsummer weather was ideal and it returned us mentally to the world of the living. The taking of Ancona less than a year before by the Second Corps had not been without suffering considerable casualties from the Wehrmacht's fighting withdrawal. Defending the city was the German 287th Infantry Division, commanded by a colorful lieutenant general by the name of Harry Hoppe. After the Poles mounted a second attack on July 17, 1944, the Germans retreated to the north the following day (Atkinson, p. 511).

The Polish Second Corps, 50,000 men under the British Eighth Army, entered the Italian theater of Allied operations from North Africa in January 1944. The Poles were engaged in battles up the eastern Adriatic coastline. Before entering Ancona, the Poles were engaged in the control of Faenza and Bologna in April. However, the best known of the Second Corps' exploits was at the protracted Battle of Monte Cassino. A total of four battles were fought over Monte Cassino by units of the U.S. Fifth Army, British Commonwealth forces, and the French, including Moroccans, with the final attack under "Operation Diadem" joined by the Second Corps. On the morning of May 18, 1944, reconnaissance elements of the Polish 12th Podolian Uhlans Regiment first broke through to the monastery two or three hours after the overnight withdrawal of the German defenders.

Giving some thought to these battles up the Italian "boot," one could not help come to the conclusion that the last thing any German soldier would want to face was surrender to the Polish army. The Germans were well aware of what the invasion and occupation of Poland meant to the Polish people caught in their grip. Polish commanders were mindful of the inclination toward revenge that existed in every one of their soldiers.

Some acts of revenge, such as combat executions, occurred before general orders, issued by corps commander General Wladyslaw Anders, filtered down to all army units. "We never take prisoners," a Polish colonel told one of the British Grenadier Guardsmen. "It's such a nuisance having to feed them and, after all they started it." "None of the Poles would hang back," as Anders later said, "for we had no men to spare for reserves. For the Polish II Corps, the way home led through the [German-claimed impenetrable] Gustav Line" (Rick Atkinson, *The Day of Battle*, p. 511).

Within a few days of the German surrender at Monte Cassino, word of the Polish army's exploits reached Warsaw. Soon there appeared on some walls in the city the painted inscription "Monte Cassino." The victory was hard fought and won. There were casualties that numbered 50 percent of Polish units committed to the campaign. The Polish cemetery is the largest of the Allied cemeteries at Monte Cassino, and at the site there is a monument, on which the following is written:

> We Polish Soldiers
> For our freedom and yours
> Have given our souls to God
> Our Bodies to the soil of Italy
> And our hearts to Poland.

As the Italians were no longer active combatants, we were told the Polish uniform was welcome among the Italian populace. That proved to be the case from our frequent off-duty visits to Ancona and Bologna. Some local citizens undoubtedly missed the largess and spending power of the Germans, since we Poles were much more frugal in our spending. Civilian clothes were not authorized, so we were required to wear our uniforms, as well as carry a holstered sidearm. Much to our frustration, all Polish personnel were forbidden to eat in local restaurants, under the rationale that local food could be poisoned. Of course this was nonsense, and it didn't stop Barbara and me from occasionally enjoying fresh fish, especially fried smelt, in two or three Ancona restaurants. Sometimes we were unable to finish our meals, having been thrown out by patrolling military police.

I had heard about a government scholarship program in England for war veterans and was encouraged to apply. I was able to acquire an application at the camp, and in surprisingly short order, I was notified that I had been accepted for a full scholarship, including living expenses, at the newly founded Polish University College at the Imperial University College in London.

Our casual time off duty was restricted somewhat by Barbara's busy surgery schedule at the field hospital. I was assigned to Colonel Skoczen's military police command, but my duties were relatively light. This afforded me time to offer my voluntary services at the hospital. One small duty I had was to oversee the kennel that housed four police dogs left behind by the Germans. They were quietly observant and very substantial in size, both German shepherds and full-size Schnauzers. No one could figure out the commands in German they were trained to obey, other than the obvious. More important, we didn't know their names. At least I figured out "attack" and "stay." I never particularly cared for dogs and had never owned one. Cats were my clear choice as a pet. I should have thanked my lucky stars for the dogs though. One big Schnauzer had a collar, with the name "Nero." At least we could address each other. Well, much to my chagrin, Nero took a liking to me and followed me everywhere in the camp. He insisted on coming to our quarters at night, so I fixed a blanket in the corner of the room for a bed.

Two or three nights later as I was getting ready for bed — fortunately Barbara was working late and was not there — the door to our quarters

Barbara Rosinski as a medical officer in the Polish Army, 1945–46.

flew open. A tall grizzled man, possibly Russian and clearly deranged, stepped into the room. He brandished a pistol while screaming at me in crude Polish: "Well, Jan, we finally meet!"

My pistol was too far away to reach, so for the moment I was trapped. "How did you get in here? There are guards all over the camp."

"It doesn't matter how. I'm going to kill you!"

"Kill me! But why, for God's sake?"

"Because you gave orders to kill 1,100 Russian agents." At this point, he stopped talking, waiting for my reaction.

My mind ground to a halt: 1,100 agents; why not just 1,000 agents? I had to say something, as he kept waving his pistol at me. Finally I managed, "You must be plainly stupid! It would take 1,100 days and maybe forever to do such a thing, and that's impossible." It seemed my quickly assembled logic wasn't working, as he ordered me to lie down on the bed. Then the accusation changed, but it was still bazaar.

"What about Samanta?"

"What about Samanta? I don't know any Samanta."

"You had to, she was your lover."

"No, I don't know any Samanta and I never had a lover. Why don't you just get the hell out of here!"

"I'll be getting out of here, but you will be staying here forever."

Suddenly it was time for me to plead, as he moved toward me and pressed the pistol to my stomach. This is where I'm thinking it's all over — my life will end in this room. "Look, you have this gun, you can shoot me whenever you want, but why don't you put it down on the table. I'm on the bed, and can't harm you, so why don't we at least talk this over?"

Jan's insignia of rank (sergeant) in the Polish Army, 1945.

Doing what I asked, he replied, "All right. So tell me about Samanta."

"I can't tell you about Samanta because I don't know anything about her. I never knew or met a Samanta in my life."

As our conversation grew louder, it finally attracted the attention of Nero, lying quietly so far in his corner bed. This was it. Live or die. I yelled out the command "fass," or "attack." Without hesitation, Nero leaped

Jan Rosinski in uniform as a Polish Army sergeant-officer candidate, 1945.

toward my would-be assailant, knocking over the table, pistol flying to the floor. Nero's launch was true to the target. He sank his teeth in the man's throat, chewing with rapid twisting motions. The dog's attack caused all sorts of commotion. Lieutenant Marian, who was a duty officer, rushed into the room, pistol drawn, demanding to know what was going on. My initial explanation wasn't particularly coherent, as Nero was still at the man's throat. Finally, Nero responded to yet another command to "stop" and retreated to his corner with blood all over his snout. Nero did what he was trained to do. It was a fantastic performance. Lt. Marian called for a doctor, who took one look at the man's neck and face and said, "He's seriously wounded. I don't think he can survive." In fact, I believe he bled to death before he could get any medical attention.

"I don't care," I said, "but let's call the MPs and get him to the hospital. Also, if you will take me to Colonel Skoczen, I'll report this matter to him." It was near midnight, but the colonel was still up, so I entered his quarters, presented the attacker's pistol and made my verbal report. Listening in total amazement, the colonel finally said, "Okay, we'll put you in a car and get you out of here. There may be others with whom this man was involved. We'll take you south to the coastal town of Bari where there's another military police unit and a colonel commanding."

"That's a good idea," I replied, "but what if I take a train and mix with the Italian people. Someone else may be observing the base here and what's going on. If you put me on a train to Trani station, just south of Barletta, then they can send a jeep to pick me up." Surprisingly, the colonel agreed and then advised they would send me to the local station in the morning.

The next morning, leaving a worried Barbara behind, I took my duffel bag and was driven, with armed escort, to the station. At least the fine fall Adriatic weather for mid–November was holding to warm temperatures. The MP officer with me talked to the Italian police at the station, and they opened a private compartment for me. Later I was joined by a kindly Italian woman who offered me a breakfast appetizer of pickled olives. Horrible! A jeep was waiting for me at the Trani station and I started my new life at the British Army camp at Bari. First, however, I had an instructive conversation with my new colonel. He apparently had known of the long record of some of my less-than-military activities that revealed my lack of patience for a regimented military life. Summing up, he told me, "Don't do anything while you are here to attract attention to yourself. I know the war is over, but we are still not discharged from service. Until then, let's just be soldiers." "Yes sir," was my obvious answer.

The colonel's rather low-key admonishment lasted overnight. The next morning I decided to launch a psychological warfare action that had been swimming in my mind for some time. My abiding hatred for Russians, in whatever guise, compelled me to launch my own such warfare before leaving military life behind. It was a long time coming, considering my father's experience living and dying in the emerging Soviet Union, my mother's long trek back to Poland through the upheaval of the Polish-Russian War of 1920, the Soviet Katyn Forest massacre in 1940 of over 21,000 Polish military officers and noncommissioned officers, and the refusal of the Soviet Army to come to the aid of Poland during the Nazis' bloody suppression of the Warsaw Uprising in the early fall of 1944.

Since I was a practiced forger, I falsified an official British Army requisition order to obtain a radio transmitter, which with some help was installed in a specially constructed hidden wall compartment in our barracks room. I had met a Polish soldier who was born in France and spoke fluent French. He accepted my offer of "temporary employment" for this special project. Again, I must confess that by now my reputation for eccentricity — craziness to some — was fairly well established. We then simulated Russian propaganda broadcasts, mostly in French and ostensibly directed at the Western Allies. Our programming had plenty of pseudo–Russian vitriol aimed at the West. At the end of each broadcast, we would quickly store the transmitter back into the wall compartment and continue with our daily routine. Soon enough, the Russians' reactions reached the British with demands to know who was speaking French and who operated the "criminal transmitter." Everything progressed well until after the third day of broadcasts. Some British officers, including a colonel, claimed that the transmissions were fabrications and coming from the area of our barracks. They walked through, searching our barracks, but found nothing, this after employing mobile radio direction-finding equipment mounted on a panel truck. They returned again two days later, and this time they had my falsified requisition order. It was now a standoff, with each side scowling at the other. The colonel finally spoke up: "Okay, where is it? We're not leaving without it!" I was clearly trapped, so I opened the wall compartment and showed him the transmitter. The next thing, the colonel held a full troop formation and ordered all French speakers to step forward and identify themselves. A few did, but not my colleague in this fast disappearing operation.

"Why didn't you step forward?" I asked.

"Are you crazy, they would probably have me arrested. I'm not that stupid."

The colonel called me into his office, puffed up and ready to invoke military discipline. He asked me several incriminating questions that I had to answer honestly. He asked what my motivation was in committing such an outlandish act. I told him frankly that one theme was paramount in my mind, and that was the consignment of Poland by the Big Three at the Yalta conference to the postwar Eastern Bloc. As a result, the Soviet Union would be in complete control of Eastern Europe. The abandonment of Poland by the British and Americans weighed heavily on my mind, and it would come back to visit me on the day Barbara and I became American citizens. But that gets ahead of my story.

Deflating somewhat, he said, "Look, I have to do something with you. For tonight, you will take a platoon of men to the Trani station and post a guard on a train there until you are relieved the next day."

My curiosity got the better of me. "Sir, what is in that train that must be guarded overnight?"

"There are all kinds of sensitive documents and records to be sent to England and I don't want anything to happen to them while they are under my command. That's it — get to it!"

My command, a whole platoon, was transported to Trani and I posted soldiers at the front and back of the train. But as the afternoon wore on, my curiosity as to what was stored in the train got the best of me. I took my pistol and shot off a lock on one of the doors. Pulling the door aside, there before my eyes were small wooden barrels labeled "Vinegar à Chateau," and below that, "Marsala." We had no tools with us, so I told one of the men to go to the nearby village and get a hammer and a few nails, which we then used to puncture a hole in one of the barrels. What came out, to our collective amazement was the most fantastic red wine. Well, I didn't drink, but in a hasty decision, I permitted the platoon to sample the wine. One of the soldiers in the platoon raced back to the camp to alert others to what had now become much more than a wine tasting event. When the news was received, a flood of soldiers made their way to Trani to take advantage of this rare opportunity. I would have to admit that this is about when I lost control of the situation.

The next morning, the colonel arrived in a three-jeep convoy with a look on his face that meant business. Virtually every soldier was either drunk or in a serious hangover. I did not drink, so I was able to stand erect and salute as the colonel stomped in my direction. "This is it!" he yelled. "I'm going to court-martial you. This will be the end of your military career, such as it is. You'll never be honorably discharged!"

I decided on the spot that the only way out of this jam was to call his bluff. "Well, you see, if we get to court, I'll merely say we were drinking vinegar because that's what the markings on the barrels said. I don't know how it will end, but I think we will probably win."

That seemed to give the colonel pause. "All right, I called your wife and told her what you have been up to."

"What did she say?"

"She laughed. We're going to send you out of here quick time. You will be put on a Royal Navy destroyer in Naples headed for Liverpool. You're going straight out of here!"

And that's what they did. My service and adventures in the European Theater of Operations had finally come to an end. Barbara would soon be sent to join me in England, and we would begin a new life never dreamed of before. However, before that, she was transferred to another hospital in Trani, which brought her closer to my camp in Bari. The colonel was interested only in seeing to my discharge from active duty. However, I had my own high motivation in going to England. While in Ancona, I had applied for the academic scholarship in physics to the Polish University College, a program sponsored by the Imperial University in London. Based on my high scholarship at the Warsaw Institute of Technology and recommendations of my professors, I received a full scholarship that included living expenses for Barbara and me. I was most fortunate, particularly since there was more than a little criticism and sensitivity in British academic circles toward such funds going to Poles rather than British citizens.

My British military superiors were aware of my university acceptance, which served to clear the way for my travel to England. Before departing for Naples, Joe Bulhak once again appeared at the camp in Bari to say goodbye to Barbara and me before going off, as he said, "on a mission to Russia." I avoided questioning him about all this, but surmised he must be engaged with the British because of his association with their SID organization. Joe also spoke fairly fluent Russian, from time spent at a family estate in Lithuania. Adding to his flair for international intrigue, Joe more than occasionally enjoyed the company of attractive women. With him on this visit of only a few hours over lunch was a dark-haired beauty and, of course, an Italian princess, who resided at a family estate near Rome. Barbara's immediate reaction was a warning to discourage my being in the presence of this delightful young woman. She had no worries there, as our marriage was quite secure.

Late in the first week of December 1945 a jeep and Italian driver was arranged to transport me to the waiting Royal Navy destroyer in Naples.

There was a priority need for Barbara to remain on the hospital's surgical staff for a few additional months. She was also nearly five month's pregnant and likely would have suffered complications on a sea-tossed navy destroyer. Another complication arose when she diagnosed herself as having early signs of ankylosing spondylitis, a terrible chronic and degenerative disorder affecting the spine and sacroiliac joints. Her diagnosis was confirmed by consultations with other doctors. As there was, and continues to be, no known cure, this disorder would eventually factor in our decision to seek some relief in a recommended dry climate in the West. My departure marked the first time we would be separated since the early days of the war in Poland and our service in the AK. It was an emotional experience and one that would not be repeated in our lives.

Just as we were ready to leave, I learned inadvertently of the location of the estate of the princess and that Joe would be there for a few days before going off on his secret escapades. Rather than take a southern route to Naples, I talked the driver into going north toward Rome, up the coastal road through Barletta, then turning southwest at Pescara through Avezzano and Tivoli. The two-day trip in an open Jeep was an adventure in itself, as the driver knew only one speed — fast. We reached the estate late in the afternoon of the second day on the road. The princess, at Joe's suggestion was kind enough to put me up at the villa with them. While still elegant in its centuries old décor, the villa did show obvious signs of the previous German occupants, a senior *Wehrmacht* general and his staff plus at least one combat command. Not wanting to overstay my welcome, and with the ship waiting, we departed on the third day down the Atlantic coast to Naples, arriving at the pier where the destroyer was berthed.

I immediately knew I was in trouble, as just looking at the ship made me seasick. I was welcomed aboard, but also mildly scolded for my late arrival. They would have departed in a few hours without me. Fortunately, I was assigned to a small cabin of my own, and that's where I remained throughout nearly all the four-day voyage. The captain was a pleasant and friendly fellow and showed considerable interest in the fact that his ship was providing special transport services to a Polish Army sergeant. I believe my personnel records were sent to the ship for transmittal to London, and he may have taken a peek. There were four other passengers aboard, but as I recall, I was the only Pole. I ended up regaling him with some stories of my various escapades in Warsaw and Italy. Finally, with a big grin on his face, he said, "You know Jan, drinking alcohol on His Majesty's ships is not allowed, but your life until now calls for a drink, so I'm inviting you to my cabin for refreshment." I still did not drink alcohol, but I couldn't refuse the captain. I suffered the next day for it, and the pitching destroyer added to my misery.

On the first day at sea, December 9, 1945, the executive officer informed us that there were still warnings or alerts on the possibility of German U-boats operating in the Mediterranean. This was strange news indeed, that after more than six months after Germany's surrender one or more U-boats could still be at war. As it turned out, we did not encounter any such threats, but we did come in contact with a submarine under the flag of Poland. What a welcome and exhilarating experience! As the destroyer was rounding the southern coast of Portugal, just outside their territorial waters, the captain informed us that they would rendezvous with a Polish submarine on a training mission and operating under overall British naval command in the Mediterranean.

I was called on deck, sick as ever, to witness the bow of the ORP *Sokol* (Republic of Poland Ship Falcon) breaking the surface, the large white designation "N97" showing prominently on the side of the conning tower. We were within shouting distance, some 50 yards, and I was given a megaphone to talk to the captain, Lieutenant Commander Tadeusz Biernas. We exchanged greetings in Polish and Biernas said that they had good hunting throughout the war and were still around to tell about it.

Barbara Rosinski with baby Mathew, Macerata, Italy, 1946.

And indeed they were. He said their biggest "kill" was an enemy troopship out of a North African port, fully loaded and no survivors. I learned later that the *Sokol* and its sister submarine, the ORP *Dzik*, were known among the allies as the "Terrible Twins." The *Sokol* flew a black "Jolly Roger" banner that displayed its record of sinkings: 22 enemy merchant ships, three warships, and 11 combat vessels, and four hostile boardings and captures. The two submarines had been leased to the Polish navy by the British Admiralty, and were to be released back to them the following year. Four other submarines acquired from the British had unfortunately been interned in neutral Swedish ports earlier in the war.

On we cruised northward, past the southern entrance to the English Channel, into the Irish Sea. Before the ship made a straight starboard swing to Liverpool, there was a final moment of excitement. On the morning of December 13 the ship's sonar picked up suspicious soundings, prompting the alert. After 30 minutes, the call to battle stations was rescinded and we continued on into Liverpool. I shared my skepticism with the captain about such threats from nonexistent U-boats. He agreed, but said he had to adhere to operating procedures in force. I could barely walk down the gangplank, being wobbly and totally unbalanced, with my duffel bag over my shoulder. I was informed on the ship that transport would be waiting for me at dockside, and that I would be taken to Kingston Camp in Herefordshire. My only reaction was, "Well, I don't know where they will be taking me, but it doesn't matter, I'll be so sick I won't be able to walk."

CHAPTER 14

England and
on to America

Despite still being plagued with seasickness, I was never so happy to be on solid ground. It was December 13, 1945. True to the captain's word, a jeep was waiting at the Liverpool dockside to take me to the British Army's Kingston Camp in Herefordshire. I bade good-bye to the captain, telling him, "I have no idea where they're taking me, but it doesn't matter, I'll be so sick, I won't be able to walk." At the headquarters building, I reported to the colonel commanding, and immediately encountered a very hostile officer. One look at me, and he blurted out, "I don't want to see you here. Just find another place to live, but stay out of this camp!"

"But sir, I have orders to stay here, and I don't know where I could go."

The colonel's secretary, a nice young woman who was a civilian employee of the Royal Navy, took pity and spoke up: "Sir, it's getting late and he needs some place to stay tonight."

"I don't care where he goes, but not here." After a pause, he retreated. "All right, there is an empty barracks at the far end of the camp. He can stay there for now."

I was taken aback by the colonel's seeming hostility toward me and wondered at its source. Perhaps he had read my records file and saw something disagreeable. Or perhaps it was an antipathy toward Poles in general. I would soon learn that such attitudes existed "on the street." While the military service of about 225,000 Poles contributed significantly to the British armed forces during the war, those of us who landed in England for resettlement or relocation were often looked on with disfavor as usurpers in a tight job market. Until benefits provided to Polish military men were

157

made available through the government-financed Polish Resettlement Corps in mid–1946, it was not uncommon for Polish men — officers included — to work as day laborers and gardeners, and at other menial chores.

There were many tragic stories of Polish soldiers stranded, in effect, in England, who could not return to their families in Poland for fear of hostile treatment by the new Soviet-backed Communist government. One such case was that of Stanislaw Maczek, commanding general of the 1st Polish Armored Division. After the war, General Maczek was deprived of his Polish citizenship and forced to remain in England. As he was not considered an Allied soldier, the British government declined to grant combatant rights and a military pension. Until the 1960s, General Maczek worked as a bartender in a hotel in Edinburgh. Still in exile, he died in England in 1994 at the age of 102. He was interned among his exiled comrades in a Polish cemetery in The Netherlands. This was as close as he was able to come to his homeland. Yet in my own experience, the British on the street offered their appreciation to a Polish soldier in uniform. Twice, as I recall, I was greeted on the street by elderly persons, both women,

Portrait of Barbara Rosinski in civilian clothes, Poland, 1938.

who happened to see the "Poland" shoulder patch on my jacket, and invited me to tea in their flat. I could hardly refuse their hospitality.

In any event, I had my own concerns for the moment. Staggering the distance with my heavy duffel bag in tow, I found my first "home" in England. It wasn't much as a soldiers barracks, and it was cold, but I didn't have to share it with 30 other men. I found a supply of wood nearby and recruited a giant of a Polish soldier to help carry an armful of cut wood and get the fire started in the one stove on the floor. After a cold meal in the camp mess, I fell into a dead sleep.

The next morning, I reported again to the headquarters. Fortunately, the colonel was not there, so I was able to appeal to his secretary for help. It was urgent for me to finalize the arrangements for my scholarship at the newly established Polish University College at the Imperial University campus in South Kingston. I explained the situation to the secretary and the necessity of preparing a travel order allowing me to go there.

"The colonel must sign such an order, and he would never do it for you," she replied.

"Well, I simply must go. Tell me, do you have any leave time to use?" She said she did, so I hatched a plot for her to write leave papers for herself, and I would use them instead, despite the obvious fact that we were of different sex.

Surprisingly, she replied, "All right, I'll see what I can do." Later that afternoon, she gave me the orders she had typed and I left the next morning.

When I got off the train at Paddington Station, I ran straight into the British military police. To compound the situation, the lone officer among them, a young lieutenant, knew me from my military police unit in Italy. "Well, what are you doing here?" he asked with a frown. I explained my purpose in coming to Kingston to arrange the papers for my scholarship at Polish University College, and then planned to return to camp.

Examining my travel papers, he quipped, "That's interesting; it seems you are now a girl."

"Well, in my business, I might have to be someone else once in a while."

That obviously didn't sell. "No matter, I must arrest you!"

"Don't be ridiculous, you will ruin my life! You can send someone with me to see that I am true to my word."

I could see he was wavering. "All right then, give me your word of honor that you will do just what you said."

I gave him my word, and miraculously, he let me go.

I was able to finalize arrangements for the scholarship and schedule without any difficulty and returned, true to my word, to the camp. When I entered the headquarters, the colonel was there and in a state of full fury. He was pacing up and down in front of the secretary, who was shaking in a state of tears. He nearly screamed at me, demanding an explanation and not waiting for one. He ordered me immediately out of the camp and to be transferred to another army base in Foxley, Herefordshire. Having expelled that out of his system, he turned abruptly and marched out of the office. In the aftermath of the storm, I could only thank this lovely woman for risking her livelihood and could only hope that she would not be punished for helping me. For her kindness, she remains in my thoughts to this day.

At the new camp, the commanding officer refused to take me. In a familiar refrain, he growled, "Just get out!" I replied that I had signed papers ordering me there, so finally he relented. I was assigned to another vacant barracks, which became my home for several months. Christmas and New Year's 1946 passed uneventfully. Admittedly, I was lonely and feeling slightly sorry for myself, although Barbara and I were lucky to be alive and with a prospect of a better life ahead. Special meals were prepared in the mess hall for those of us "trapped," so there were still some benefits of my army status. Also, fortunately for us, Barbara and I could occasionally use a telephone link directly from her hospital in Trani, Italy, and the main phone in the headquarters building of my camp.

Later in January, classes started at the Polish University College. Imperial University College had allocated one building on campus for our college. It housed lecture rooms and a laboratory. It was a modest, but welcome, start. The first class totaled not more than about 25 men, but others would follow. It was a relaxed and rewarding time for me. Academia was where I belonged and I found that I retained unusual passion for the challenge of examinations. At the end of the first year I was given an award for academic excellence and a small prize. I also supplemented my course work by occasionally attending lectures given by a professor and a graduate researcher at Cambridge University. Ronald Norrish held the distinguished position of professor of physical chemistry for nearly 30 years and was assisted by George Porter, who later was appointed to a full professorship. Their collaboration culminated in sharing the Nobel Prize for chemistry in 1967 for their work in fast reactions. I greatly appreciated the personal attention given to me by Professor Norrish. Perhaps it was my army uniform that attracted his attention initially. He had served in the Grenadier Guards during World War I and had been a prisoner in Germany toward the end of the war.

The telephone call from Barbara in Trani, Italy, that I had been waiting for came on April 28, 1946. In a weak voice, she told me we had a son, Mathew. Baby and mother were doing just fine. What a relief to know all was well. They could not travel to England for three or four months, so my wait for my family began. In the meantime, a major event in England was approaching, much to the frustration and sensitivity of every Pole who had served with the Allied armed forces. Long in advance, the government of Prime Minister Clement Atlee had invited representatives of all Allied forces for a victory parade in London on June 8, 1946. All, that is, except the Polish armed forces that had fought gallantly beside Great Britain from the early days of the Battle of Britain. The government was sensitized to the Soviet hostility toward a free Poland in general and the contribution Polish free forces made to the Allied effort. Chairman Joseph Stalin was not to be insulted. All my colleagues at the university and in the army took this as a personal affront. I decided to organize a small social event at the university while thousands marched along the Mall in central London.

On a grey and damp day, some 20,000 strong from more than 10 nations, led by a large contingent of American troops and brought up in the rear of the mile-long line, were 10,000 men and women of Great Britain's armed forces marching along the Mall. Among those watching from along the parade route were some of us veterans of the Polish army, air force, and navy — in total the fourth largest manpower contribution to the Allied war effort against Hitler's Germany. One young Polish pilot from the famous Kosciuszko 303 Squadron looked on in silence while the parade passed. Then he turned to walk away. An old woman standing next to him looked at him quizzically. "Why are you crying, young man?" she asked. The squadron had led the aerial defense in the Battle of Britain, downing 14 German aircraft on the first day. In its first eight days of combat, the squadron destroyed nearly forty enemy planes. Initially, the Polish pilots flew Hawker Hurricanes, and later Spitfires as they became available (Olson and Cloud, pp. 4, 6).

Finally, in early July, Barbara called to alert me that she had secured passage on a special train reserved for Polish military personnel and dependents from 2nd Army Headquarters in Italy to the French port of Calais on the English Channel and then to Dover, England, via ferry. The arrangements and cost for the transportation were provided by the Australian and New Zealand armed forces. I don't recall the exact date of travel, but it was in late July or early August. There were confusing messages along the travel route and arrival at Calais. There were also further delays there, as a reception group waited at Dover with buses and British officials to assist in directing the passengers to temporary living quarters.

Finally the ferry arrived at the Dover docks, and the most bizarre story of misadventure unfolded before those of us waiting. It is quite likely that some of what occurred along the train route was hushed up for security reasons, but enough came out to enrage all of us. Although the train was reserved exclusively for Polish personnel, a group of Ukrainian men, their numbers unknown but presumably veterans from either the Russian or German army, had smuggled themselves aboard the train by bribing the train crew. Likely in a drunken state, they proceeded to harass passengers and create utter havoc. In an apparent frenzy, they even took knives and slashed the seats. Miraculously, neither Barbara nor Mathew was attacked, as some passengers were, but Barbara was severely traumatized and suffered severe abdominal pains. Fortunately, even though she was discharged from the army before her departure from Trani, she had decided to wear her officer's uniform as perhaps a means of giving her added security or official status during the long trip.

I was shocked to see her being carried on a stretcher off the ferry and Mathew in the arms of a Polish woman. It was a hectic scene at the dock. One woman passenger became nearly crazy with grief from the death of her son on the train. A fight broke out between a British officer and a Polish colonel over a question of authority in transporting the passengers. A quick decision was made by British officers to transport Barbara immediately to a hospital in Liverpool. She remained there for two weeks. Fortunately, we were helped by one Polish officer, Major Larko, and his daughter. The major and his family had found civilian housing close to my camp and were able to arrange a temporary flat for the three of us. So I was able to move out of the barracks and finally live as a civilian — except, that is, for my uniform, which I still wore. Major Larko's daughter took a fancy to Mathew and helped us to buy baby food and even a baby stroller for taking Mathew out for excursions around the neighborhood. Several months later, the Larko family, at my suggestion, emigrated to Argentina. I had heard about a limited Polish resettlement plan promoted by the Argentine embassy in London and had made inquiries for my own interest.

Since this housing arrangement was only temporary or on an emergency basis, it soon became time to search for a longer-term flat. It seemed that Barbara and I walked the streets of London forever, knocking on doors in search of a place to live. The problem was that no one was willing to rent to a family with a young child. Finally, in an upscale neighborhood on Elm Park Gardens, we found unexpected good fortune. Answering the doorbell was a middle-aged woman, stylishly dressed, who scrutinized us closely. This is understandable, since there we stood, two foreign army persons and a child. It was her sympathy for Mathew that got us in the door. She introduced herself as Mrs. Champion and explained that she was living only with her daughter Mary. Her husband, a Royal Navy officer, had been killed in a Japanese naval battle. She had taken a liking to us, and we immediately accepted her offer of a basement apartment. The agreement was sealed by Mrs. Champion buying a rocking horse for

Mathew. As time passed, we became quite friendly. She offered me a position as an overseer on a plantation she owned in Jamaica, which I respectfully declined. She would ask again, but she finally accepted my explanation that I needed to complete my scholarship studies and move on in my future career in chemistry. (There was only one very sensitive incident that occurred that could have disturbed our friendship with Mrs. Champion. We had not met her daughter Mary yet, so when we happened to see or meet her and a friend in a quite compromising situation she did not know us, nor we her. When we did meet at the house, Mary was in a state of shock. After collecting her wits, she begged us to keep what had passed between us a secret. This I honored my entire life.)

In mid–1946 the British government announced the formation of the Polish Resettlement Corp, or PRC. It was established to assist members of the Polish armed forces in relocating in England and finding at least temporary employment. Monthly stipends were also provided for living expenses based on military rank as well as vocational training. It was a two-year program and members were still regarded as military personnel and subject to British military discipline. I entered the corps in December 1946 and stayed until discharged in December 1948. The program was terminated in 1949. It became controversial in some British political circles, especially some of the trade unions that claimed nonmember Poles were taking better jobs away from their members. Yet, there was no question that it saved many Polish veterans from destitution.

In the same month I signed up for the PRC, I was discharged from the regular army. At the end of November, I was ordered to the camp headquarters and a major informed me of the situation and advised that I would be discharged in about seven to ten days. "In the meantime," he admonished, "you are free to do whatever you want to do, but for heavens sake don't do anything crazy!"

On December 5, 1948, the day of discharge arrived, and I reported to the staff officer on duty, saluting and giving my name and rank for the last time. Somewhat studiously, he looked at me in puzzlement. "I'm just going through your records, and do you know what they were thinking?" I had no response. "They were concerned that you might be a Russian spy. There are pages and pages in here of your activities — whatever you were doing — perhaps to destroy our army. But, it's all upside down. Tell me one thing. How did you manage to get that radio transmitter?"

"Well, it was simple. I forged the necessary documents and I got it. I had British soldiers load it for me on a truck and deliver it to the barracks."

"Really! That is amazing." After a long pause, he said, "Okay, I'm going to give you some advice. Don't go back to the university. Don't go back to school. Just get out of here, go somewhere and write your memoirs. I guarantee it will be a best seller. Then you won't have to go back to school and study. You can live off of your book profits."

"Thank you sir for your advice, but I must finish my chemistry degree, and I cannot write at all. I'm not a writer." He seemed to accept my reasoning, and that ended our conversation. It also ended my military career and this is how I departed from the Polish 2nd Corps.

However, before I left for London, I was awarded a medal, for what exploits I am uncertain. The colonel managed to comport himself for the occasion and pinned it on my tunic. As I was leaving the headquarters, I was trying to adjust the angle of the pinned medal. A couple with a young boy happened to be walking by. The boy seemed attracted to my uniform and shinny new medal. With bright eyes, he told me he hoped to have such a medal one day. I replied, "Would you like to have it?" He jumped with excitement, so I unpinned the medal and handed it to him. He ran back to his parents overjoyed with his good luck. When I returned from the headquarters, Barbara was waiting for me. "Let me see what they gave to you."

"Well, I received a medal, but I no longer have it, and I explained what had just happened.

"Jan, this is just like you!"

I still don't know what the medal was for. Perhaps when I grow even older I'll begin to wonder what the citation read. For now, however, the question remains unanswered.

Before the year was out, I had one important mission to attempt. I was determined to find out what I could about the probable association of my uncle Jozef Rosinski and my deceased friend Edward Rossenberg with British intelligence, more specifically the Secret Intelligence Service (SIS) or MI6. I made inquiries about their headquarters in London, and finally the police advised me of an office, if not their headquarters, on Downing Street, not far, as it turned out, from the prime minister's residence at No. 10. On the appointed morning, I approached the building protected by a strong fence-work. There were no uniformed guards, but I observed two or three husky-looking fellows in civilian suits and coats. As I was in uniform, I was allowed to enter, only to be confronted by a healthy-looking male receptionist. I introduced myself and explained my interest in discussing their past activities in Poland as they related to my uncle and friend. While I evoked a certain sympathy in mentioning my service in the Polish underground, my efforts to acquire even a modest amount of information were not meeting with success. Two officials were summoned to the lobby, and, while showing perfunctory interest, they were not particularly helpful. Finally, I was pointedly asked to leave. I thought of resisting and pressing my case further, but then some British army officer would then be alerted and would have to bail me out. So, the wartime lives of these two men will, of necessity, remain secret.

There is one more old friend whose life after the underground days will remain a mystery. Dates escape me, but while in my early term at the university, I was tipped off by a classmate that Joe Bulhak was in London and in trouble. After making hectic inquiries, I learned that he was being held at a police station in central London. I made my way there the same afternoon, planting myself in front of the desk sergeant. Here again my uniform got me in the door, but the police still seemed confused about just who Joe was. I gave them some information about our past association in Warsaw and with the Polish army in Italy, which seemed to lessen the puzzle over Joe. It now appeared he was being held more for his own safety than as some crime suspect. The police sergeant finally brought Joe out of a back room and we greeted each other with hefty hugs. Before I squeezed the story of this escapade from him, he advised me that he had given the police a special contact number in London and he expected to be released within an hour or two.

Joe was not in a particularly talkative mood, and this is as much as he would reveal: Outside a London pub the previous night, he had been attacked by two men, East European, or possibly Russian, wielding a lead pipe. With his super-human strength, Joe was able to wrench the pipe from them and then beat them both to death right on the sidewalk. The police were summoned, of course, and he was quickly taken to the station. That is all of the incident he would speak of, and it was up to the authorities to investigate the identity of his attackers. Joe smiled and confided he would be leaving soon for the U.S. as "Mr. West," a name he had selected himself. He then told me in a hushed voice that he would also be going to Russia. That was all he would say, and, under the circumstances, I did not press him any further. Wherever his adventures took him, I'm sure he survived to old age. I suspect he may have returned to Poland after the communist regime was turned out, but I have not been able to find him.

The routine of daily living finally settled in for Barbara, me and our son, Mathew. The years of 1947 and early 1948 were uneventful and peaceful, for which we were thankful. I graduated from Polish University College

Jan Rosinski in the Chocholowska Valley, Tatra Mountains, 2000.

with an honors degree in chemistry the summer of 1948. As I was now self-supporting, I was also discharged, on December 5, 1948, from the Polish Resettlement Corp. Finally, I could take off my nearly tattered army uniform I had worn throughout my university days and enter real civilian life. I was immediately offered a job as a research chemist with British Celanese, Ltd., in Spondon, Derby, which I held until the spring of 1951. During my employment, Barbara and I came to the decision that our

Jan Rosinski at the Warsaw Uprising Monument, Krasinski Square, Warsaw, 2000.

future would be in America. Most important was Barbara's medical condition, which was not subsiding. The English weather impacted negatively on Barbara's ankylosing spondylitis, which necessitated her occasional use of a wheelchair. For me, my future as a chemist could best be pursued in the U.S., where there were greater research opportunities. My English was now professionally fluent, so it was logical to seek a new life in an English-speaking country. Also, I had been offered a position in Chicago as chief chemist with Poray, Inc., by its owner, a wealthy Polish-American entrepreneur by the name of Poranski. He was generous in his offer, which included housing and vacation time in Florida. At the same time, his demands were considerable, and he all but expected a lifetime commitment to building his firm — from its concentration on metal finishing technology — and expanding research. Some of Poray's contracts were of a classified nature with the U.S. government.

Barbara and I were well received by the consular officers at the American embassy in London and our application for immigration, along with proof of employment, was accepted without delay. Fortunately, as part of my benefits, the Polish Resettlement Corps covered the expense for travel by boat to the U.S. So it was that the little Rosinski family, having said farewell to professors and friends, departed Liverpool on a breezy April morning in 1951 on a British liner bound for New York. The five days at sea were not the most pleasant for me, but without doubt they were considerably better than my previous sea voyage on a Royal Navy destroyer. As the boat approached the harbor, we went to the port railing, and, like millions of immigrants before us, gazed out at Ellis Island and the magnificent Statue of Liberty. Someone asked us years later if we found the moment to be emotional. Off course we were elated, but we did not cry with tears of joy. All our tears had been shed years before. On arrival in New York we took transport to Union Station and from there a train directly to Chicago. Our lives in America would take us later to Boulder, Colorado, and my advanced research with the National Center for Atmospheric Research (NCAR), and part-time work with the National Oceanographic and Atmospheric Administration (NOAA). For now, however, we were home at last.

On July 17, 1956, a swelteringly hot day in Chicago, the Rosinski family took the oath of citizenship in the U.S. District Court for Northern Illinois. It was a proud day for us, but at the same time our now previous Polish nationality and memories of war and turmoil would be with Barbara and me for all the years to come. Yet this day would not be without an unexpected conversation with the presiding judge. While sitting in the courtroom with the many other new citizens, we were approached by the clerk of the court. He informed us politely that it was the judge's custom to invite a representative new citizen to have some refreshments with him in his chambers. Thinking momentarily of the worst, we walked hesitatingly into his chambers to face the smiling judge, who immediately put us at ease. He explained his personal social protocol and asked some questions about Poland and our experiences in coming to America. Then finally he remarked that, as Poles, we must be grateful for what the United States and President Roosevelt had done for Poland in the war and how grateful we must be to have received such critical support.

I was momentarily stunned. I could simply not comprehend what I had just heard and I am afraid my occasional tendency to outspokenness got the best of me. I reminded the judge that it was President Roosevelt who consigned Poland to Communism and the newly formed Soviet bloc in Central Europe. I reminded him of World War II history and what occurred at the Yalta Conference in February 1945, when the dictator Stalin demanded hegemony over Poland and had gotten his way. Prime Minister Churchill and President Roosevelt gave Poland away to the East and turned their backs on the widespread purges that followed. I was quite prepared to continue my lecture, but Barbara reached across, touched my arm and

Jan in the Tatra Mountains, Morskie Oko, 2000.

in curt Polish admonished me: "Jan, for God's sake, don't say anything more, or we'll never become American citizens." Fortunately, the judge appeared not to take my blunt remarks personally, and our presence at the courthouse continued without incident. We were finally citizens of a free country.

Epilogue

It has been 58 years since my family and I arrived to take up our new life in America and 47 years since we made our home in Boulder, Colorado. The first 11 years we spent in Chicago where I was chief chemist at Poray Inc. and then senior scientist in the Department of Chemistry at Armour Research Foundation in the Illinois Institute of Technology. In 1962, due to Barbara's poor health, we moved to Boulder, Colorado. The dry mountain climate helped to restore some improvement in Barbara's ongoing struggle with ankylosing spondylitis. My work as a physicist and chemist in atmospheric sciences proved rewarding in several research projects. During my years at the National Center for Atmospheric Research (NCAR) and the National Oceanographic and Atmospheric Administration (NOAA), I received three research patents, all assigned to federal government agencies, and published over 110 research papers, individually and jointly with colleagues. Much of this research focused primarily on the physics of severe storms, especially the formation of rain and hail. On many occasions I lectured at the University of Toronto, Canada, universities in Rome, Ferrara and Bologna, Italy, as well as the University of Warsaw. I was also presented in 2002 with the Petr Beckmann Award by Doctors for Disaster Preparedness: "For courage and achievement in defense of scientific truth and freedom."

I returned to Warsaw in 1976 for the first time in 32 years to receive a Ph.D. in physics from the University of Warsaw. Although my mother had visited us for one year in Chicago in 1956, it was our first meeting in Poland since September 1944 when we both were forced to separate German prisoner camps. The scars of war were still visible throughout the city, and a reminder that war was not too far behind us, nor possibly not too far in the future as a hostage between East and West blocs. Somewhat to my surprise, I was not confronted with interference from the communist regime's security police. Nevertheless, I was advised not to stay with my mother, so as not to call unnecessary attention to her. So I stayed in a hotel and, with available time, enjoyed several family dinners and gatherings.

I had made one previous trip to Italy in 1968 to receive an academic title, L.D. (Libera Docenca), in atmospheric physics from the University of Bologna. With the encouragement and help of my good Italian friend Professor Ottavio Vittori, I also won an international competition for an academic chair at the University of Bologna in chemistry and physics of the atmosphere. Ottavio was a frequent visitor to our home in Boulder, where he was always welcome. He often sought Barbara's advice and counsel on personal and religious matters. Her discussions with him, in context of our Catholic faith, drew us particularly close and he became like family to us.

In 1980 I received a postdoctorate (Doctor Habilitatus) from the University of Warsaw and enjoyed several meetings with professors at Warsaw University and also the Warsaw Institute of Technology. Another trip in 2000 proved most interesting. The primary purpose of my travel was to perform experiments with Italian scientists at the ISAO Institute of Physics in Bologna, which then took me to Warsaw for a personal visit. I was invited by Zosia Gasienica-Gladczan, my old AK contact in the Tatra Mountain town of Zakopane. Zosia had survived the underground war without threats to her safety and had been widowed a few years earlier. We took particular delight in recalling our prewar meetings and companionship when we would take hiking trips in the mountains. With the help of the Tatra Mountains Rescue, my friend Dr. Grazyna A. Kras during my visit organized many spectacular trips to the higher areas of the Tatra Mountains. On one trek, we visited Kasprowy Wierch, a very popular mountain ski area where in the early winter of 1942 I had been confronted by a German officer, Josef Jennewein,

Jan Rosinski, professor, Ph.D., senior scientist, National Center for Atmospheric Research (NCAR), Boulder, Colorado, 1998.

a Luftwaffe pilot and Austrian by birth who undoubtedly saved me from arrest by the Gestapo. Zosia and I also reminisced about the German soldier artist we both helped to desert from a likely fate in the Stalingrad campaign. Zosia had led him into the forest outside Zakopane on the first leg of his journey and then turned him over to another unit of the AK. Because of our strict procedure on secrecy and compartmentation, she knew nothing more of his fate.

The year 1993 was a bleak one, as my beloved wife, Barbara, finally succumbed to a tragic disorder that had plagued her for many years. Our home had become a medical care facility as a hospital bed was moved into the living room; and our daily routines, as well as my research work, were planned around her needs. Her bravery and cheer in the face of this challenge was something of a wonder. My oncoming blindness progressed soon thereafter and became a growing threat to my devotion to scientific research.

My last trip to Poland in the summer of 2008 had best not been taken. The day after my arrival in Warsaw I suffered a stroke and was hospitalized for 18 days and then spent two weeks in a rehabilitation sanatorium. I was fortunate to be helped by my caregiver and close friend, Dr. Grazyna Anna Kras, who traveled with me on this trip and on the previous trip in 2000. Upon my release, and now in a wheelchair, I had brief visits with two cousins. On my last day there, I was interviewed for an hour at the Warsaw Rising Museum about my experiences in the underground. The interview was conducted by a museum employee and videotaped. Still feeling the effects of the stroke, it was not my best performance.

Looking back, the many trips and projects, the Ph.D. exams in Warsaw and Italy, the many joint ventures, establishing new scientific experimental stations on several continents, and lecturing at various universities gave me the opportunity to work with many scientists of world renown. Noteworthy among them were Professor Chris Junge, director of the Max Planck Institute in Mainz, Germany, Professor Ottavio Vittori of Italy, Professor Swinbank of Australia, and Dr. Walter Roberts of NCAR in Boulder, Colorado.

In 1957, I was honored to receive an invitation to attend a meeting in the White House. President Eisenhower wished to personally thank the research scientists who had made contributions to national defense projects. He was most gracious in his remarks. Caught up in the moment, I completely forgot to tell him I had a personal possession of his that I could have returned to him. Twelve years earlier, during a train ride while I was still in Italy in uniform, I met an American sergeant who was at the time

General Eisenhower's personal aide. In appreciation for his service, the general had given the sergeant his favorite walking stick. I was surprised when the sergeant, in turn, offered it to me. Even now, it rests in the corner of my study.

My last journey to Warsaw brought an end to my travels outside the U.S. After two minor strokes, my world is now restricted to Boulder. Grazyna takes me to further rehabilitation sessions and for short walks. I enjoy riding in the car with her and even an outing for mushrooming and fishing in mountain forests. A cat we named "Zuzia," or Susie, has become a worthy replacement for "Puss" and helps relieve my world of blindness. Fortunately, I still have my humor and a lifelong trust in God. Someone asked me what final thoughts I might have from my wartime experiences. Perhaps it can best be said that every morning I prayed to survive the day and every evening I prayed that I had survived the day.

Jan Rosinski passed away peacefully at his home in Boulder, Colorado, on February 25, 2012. The funeral service was held for him at Sacred Heart of Mary Catholic Church on March 3, 2012. The service was attended by a large number of friends, neighbors and colleagues in the scientific community. He was laid to rest alongside the grave of his beloved wife, Barbara. A few close colleagues in science offered personal remarks about Jan's remarkable career spanning nearly 70 years. At the grave site, a representative of the Polish diplomatic mission in the U.S. spoke briefly about Jan's place in Polish history during World War II. I offered a few comments about Jan and Barbara's "other life" during World War II. I could see that many gathered there were undoubtedly surprised upon hearing about Jan's secret underground life.

Two weeks later, a candlelight mass was held for Jan's memory at the university church, Saint Thomas Aquinas, in Boulder. Jan's passing was also noted in Warsaw by family and friends, as well as by some Polish scientists who worked with Jan on research projects. A memorial mass was held in the Field Cathedral of the Polish Army in Warsaw. Soil, symbolically gathered from Jan's grave, and a special black marble plate honoring him were put in place on his mother's grave in Powazki, the oldest cemetery in Warsaw, Poland.

Bibliography

Atkinson, Rick. *The Day of Battle: The War in Sicily and Italy, 1943–1944*. New York: Henry Holt, 2007.

Davies, Norman. *Rising '44: The Battle for Warsaw*. New York: Viking, 2004.

Giziowski, Richard. *Enigma of General Blaskowitz*. Hippocrine Books, 1996.

Karski, Jan. *Story of a Secret State: My Report to the World*. 1944. London: Penguin, 2011.

Olson, Lynn, and Stanley Cloud. *A Question of Honor: The Kosciuszko Squadron; Forgotten Heroes of World War II*. New York: Knopf, 2003.

Read, Anthony. *The Devil's Disciples: Hitler's Inner Circle*. New York: W.W. Norton, 2004.

Shirer, William L. *The Rise and Fall of the Third Reich: A History of Nazi Germany*. New York: Simon & Schuster, 1960.

Index

Numbers in *bold italics* indicate pages with photographs.